TAMING THE TONGUE

Bert Ghezzi and Peter Williamson
General Editors

Taming the Tongue

*Why Christians Should Care
About What They Say*

Mark Kinzer

SERVANT BOOKS
Ann Arbor, Michigan

Published by Servant Books, Box 8617, Ann Arbor, Michigan 48107

Cover photo and book design by John B. Leidy. Cover photo copyright © 1982 by Servant Publications.

Most scripture quotations in this book are taken from the *Revised Standard Version*, copyright 1946, 1953 © 1971, 1973 by the Division of Christian Education of the National Council of the Churches of Christ in the U.S.A.

ISBN 0-89283-165-0
Printed in the United States of America

Contents

Living as a Christian

IN HUMAN TERMS, it is not easy to decide to follow Jesus Christ and to live our lives as Christians. Jesus requires that we surrender our selves to him, relinquish our aspirations for our lives, and submit our will to God. Men and women have never been able to do this easily; if we could, we wouldn't need a savior.

Once we accept the invitation and decide to follow Jesus, a new set of obstacles and problems assert themselves. We find that we are often ignorant about what God wants of us as his sons and daughters. For example, what does it mean practically to obey the first commandment—to love God with our whole mind, heart, and strength? How can we know God's will? How do we love people we don't like? How does being a Christian affect what we do with our time and money? What does it mean "to turn the other cheek?" In these areas—and many others—it is not easy to understand exactly what God wants.

Even when we do know what God wants, it can be quite difficult to apply his teaching to our daily lives. Questions abound. How do we find time to pray regularly? How do we repair a relationship with someone we have wronged or who has wronged us? How do we handle unruly emotional reactions? These are examples of perplexing questions about the application of Christian teaching to our daily lives.

Furthermore, we soon discover that Christians have enemies—the devil outside and the flesh within. Satan tempts us to sin; our inner urges welcome the temptation, and we find our will to resist steadily eroding.

Finally, we must overcome the world. We are trying to live in an environment that is hostile toward what Christians believe and how they live and friendly toward those who believe and do the opposite. The world in which we live works on our Christian resolve in many subtle ways. How much easier it is to think and act like those around us! How do we persevere?

There is a two-fold answer to these questions: To live successfully as Christians, we need both grace and wisdom. Both are freely available from the Lord to those who seek him.

As Christians we live by grace. The very life of God works in us as we try to understand God's teaching, apply it to our lives, and overcome the forces that would turn us aside from our chosen path. The grace we need is always there. The Lord is with us always, and the supply of his grace is inexhaustible.

Yet grace works with wisdom. Christians must *learn* a great deal about how to live according to

God's will. We must study God's word in scripture, listen to Christian teaching, and reflect on our own experience and the experience of others. Many Christians today lack this kind of wisdom. This is the need which the *Living as a Christian* series is designed to meet.

The book you are reading is part of a series of books intended to help Christians apply the teaching of scripture to their lives. The authors of *Living as a Christian* books are pastoral leaders who have given this teaching in programs of Christian formation in various Christian communities. The teaching has stood the test of time. It has already helped many people grow as faithful servants of the Lord. We decided it was time to make this teaching available in book form.

All the *Living as a Christian* books seek to meet the following criteria:

- **Biblical.** The teaching is rooted in scripture. The authors and editors maintain that scripture is the word of God, and that it ought to determine what Christians believe and how they live.

- **Practical.** The purpose of the series is to offer down-to-earth advice about living as a Christian.

- **Relevant.** The teaching is aimed at the needs we encounter in our daily lives—at home, in school, on the job, in our day-to-day relationships.

- **Brief and Readable.** We have designed the series for busy people from a wide variety of backgrounds. Each of the authors presents profound Christian truths as simply and clearly as possible, and illustrates those truths by examples drawn from personal experience.

- **Integrated.** The books in the series comprise a unified curriculum on Christian living. They do not present differing views, but rather they take a consistent approach.

The format of the series makes it suitable for both individual and group use. The books in *Living as a Christian* can be used in such group settings as Sunday school classes, adult education programs, prayer groups, classes for teen-agers, women's groups, and as a supplement to Bible study.

The *Living as a Christian* series is divided into several sets of books, each devoted to a different aspect of Christian living. These sets include books on Christian maturity, emotions in the Christian life, the fruit of the Holy Spirit, Christian personal relationships, Christian service, and, very likely, on other topics as well.

This book, *Taming the Tongue,* is part of a set that deals with Christian personal relationships. All of us have relationships with other Christians; we worship, work, socialize, and live with them. Often, these relationships do not work as well as they should. We need to improve them—to control our speech, to offer constructive correction, to handle conflict wisely. Many of us must help other Christians improve their relationships, as well as improve our own. *Taming the Tongue* and other books in this set explain the scriptural teaching about relationships, and show how we can apply it.

The editors dedicate the *Living as a Christian* series to Christian men and women everywhere who have counted the cost and decided to follow Jesus Christ as his disciples.

Bert Ghezzi and Peter Williamson
General Editors

Preface

I BEGAN MY WORK on this book by collating and studying the main passages in the Old and New Testaments that contain instruction in godly speech. This task proved more challenging than I had first supposed or hoped; I ended up with over two hundred passages requiring scrutiny. As I meditated on them, I became more convinced than ever of the importance of righteous speech in the biblical view of the Christian life. The biblical teaching on speech is thorough, unified, and eminently practical. A diligent application of this teaching will have a profound impact on our personal relationships and daily lives.

In the following pages I quote liberally from an ancient Jewish book of wisdom usually known as the book of Sirach (it is also called Ecclesiasticus). This book forms part of what Protestants call the aprocrypha and Roman Catholics call the deuterocanonical works. Whereas Roman Catholics regard Sirach as part of holy scripture, Protestants generally view it as instructive and upbuilding, but not part of the inspired and authoritative biblical canon. No judgment on this question is implied in the present volume. Sirach offers much helpful wisdom on the topic of speech—wisdom that Protestants can appreciate as well as Roman

Catholics. He also contributes a good measure of entertainment, which I hope you will enjoy as much as I do.

ONE

"Death and Life Are in the Power of the Tongue"

B Y YOUR WORDS you will be justified, and by your words you will be condemned" (Mt 12:37). Our words are of tremendous importance. In fact, speech is one of the most crucial areas of practical Christian teaching, if sheer volume of related scripture passages is any measure. God is intensely concerned with the quality—and the quantity—of our words. This concern contrasts starkly with the undiscerning and undiscerned sea of words that daily threatens to drown us in twentieth-century America.

All too often modern Christians fail to recognize the full depth, scope, and seriousness of the biblical teaching on speech. This leaves us vulnerable to the disordered patterns of speech found in our secular environments—gossip, detraction, slander, rudeness, indiscretion, complaining, and biting humor. Relationships suffer and conflicts abound as these patterns begin to dominate our conversation. We lose the bond of peace that should guard and embody the unity of the Spirit (Eph 4:3). All this could be avoided by a sounder understanding and application of the biblical teaching on speech.

The flood of words unleashed in our society by the constantly expanding communications media need not carry us along like a floating log, dissolving all powers of moral discrimination. Similarly, our speech need not be molded and shaped by a network of non-Christian work associates or neighbors. Instead, our speech should be placed under the rule of Jesus Christ, to bear fruit for his kingdom.

The Power of the Word

The reason God is so concerned with our speech is because of its great power. Our words are capable of great good or great harm: "Death and life are in the power of the tongue" (Prv 18:21). If our tongues are submitted to the authority of God, they will bring life, both to others and to ourselves. If our tongues are restless, untamed, and rebellious, they will bring death.

Let us now look at what scripture teaches about the power of speech. We begin at the beginning— Genesis 1. "And God *said,* 'Let there be light'; and there was light" (1:3). How does God create the world? It is through his *word.* "By the word of the Lord the heavens were made, and all their host by the breath of his mouth. . . . For he spoke, and it came to be; he commanded, and it stood forth" (Ps 33:6, 9). When God speaks a word, he does not merely communicate information; the word of

God is a word of power, effectively accomplishing the purpose for which it is sent (Is 55:11). When God speaks, things happen.

God then proceeds to express his authority over that which he has made by giving it a name: "God called the light Day, and the darkness he called Night" (1:5). In Hebrew, as in English, one names an object by "calling it" something—by speaking of it or to it. In Hebrew the expression "give a name" (2:20) is literally "call a name." God names the light Day, the darkness Night, the firmament Heaven, the dry land Earth, the water Seas. Thus God expresses his authority by speaking words which define the various elements of his creation and imprint upon them their distinctive character.

The making of man on the sixth day culminates the work of creation. "Let us make man in our image, after our likeness; and let them have dominion over the fish of the sea, and over the birds of the air, and over the cattle, and over all the earth, and over every creeping thing that creeps upon the earth" (1:26). God creates man in his own image and likeness that he may rule as his representative over the earth. The first expression of man's unique nature and his share in God's image and authority occurs later, in chapter 2:

So out of the ground the Lord God formed every beast of the field and every bird of the air, and brought them to the man to see what he would call them; and whatever the man called every living creature, that was its name. The

man gave names to all cattle, and to the birds of
the air, and to every beast of the field. (2:19-20a)

God had given man the capacity to speak—a gift
given to no other animal—that man might participate in his divine nature and authority. Man's first
act of governance is to "call the names" of the
animals, thereby assuming his place as their
rightful ruler.

The power of speech is further emphasized in
the narrative of the tower of Babel found in
Genesis 11:1-9. The first family had disobeyed
God in the garden, and the human race had
degenerated into pride, violence, and sexual immorality. But human beings still had a share in the
divine image (Gn 9:6), and still were capable of
exercising a measure of authority—though not
always for the good.

Now the whole earth had one language and few
words. And as men migrated from the east, they
found a plain in the land of Shinar and settled
there. And they said to one another, "Come, let
us make bricks, and burn them thoroughly."
And they had brick for stone, and bitumen for
mortar. Then they said, "Come, let us build
ourselves a city, and a tower with its top in the
heavens, and let us make a name for ourselves,
lest we be scattered abroad upon the face of the
whole earth." And the Lord came down to see
the city and the tower, which the sons of men

had built. And the Lord said, "Behold, they are one people, and they have all one language; and this is only the beginning of what they will do; and nothing that they propose to do will be impossible for them. Come, let us go down, and there confuse their language, that they may not understand one another's speech." So the Lord scattered them abroad from there over the face of all the earth, and they left off building the city. Therefore its name was called Babel, because there the Lord confused the language of all the earth; and from there the Lord scattered them abroad over the face of all the earth.

One of the greatest advantages homo sapiens have over other animal species is their complex system of social and cultural organization. And the heart of this system is the word—the subtle and adaptable method of communication unique to humans. The people of Babel, inflated by a pride and ambition tinged with insecurity, build a powerful city and a high tower, demonstrating the corporate mastery they still possess as an inheritance from God. God's response to their enterprise is enlightening: "Behold, they are one people, and they have all one language; and this is only the beginning of what they will do; and nothing that they propose to do will be impossible for them." Unity is in itself a good thing, but it can also serve dangerous and evil ends. The fallen human race

had too much power in its hands—and so God
stepped in and confused their tongues, provoking
disunity and frustrating the human attempt to
gain total mastery. Witness again the power of the
word.

The power of words is again illustrated in the
biblical understanding of blessing and cursing.
Words of blessing and cursing in scripture do not
merely express benevolent hopes or malevolent
wishes; instead, they actually accomplish and
ensure the very reward, good or evil, which they
promise—at least if they are pronounced by one in
a position of proper authority, such as a father, a
prophet, or a priest. This explains the elaborate
ruse conducted by Jacob in order to steal his
father's blessing from his brother Essau. These are
the words pronounced by Isaac over the one he
mistakenly believed to be his eldest son: "Let
peoples serve you, and nations bow down to you.
Be lord over your brothers, and may your mother's
sons bow down to you. Cursed be every one who
curses you, and blessed be everyone who blesses
you" (Gn 27:29). The words were spoken with
power, and they could not be withdrawn, even
though Jacob received the blessing under a false
pretense:

When Esau heard the words of his father, he
cried out with an exceedingly great and bitter
cry, and said to his father, "Bless me, even me
also, O my father!" But he said, "Your brother

came with guile, and he has taken away your blessing." (Gn 27:34-35)

How does Isaac view the blessing he has just given to Jacob? Isaac has not merely wished Jacob well, but has delivered to him a tangible gift that cannot be taken away. To Esau, Isaac said, "Behold, I have made him your lord, and all his brothers I have given to him for servants, and with grain and wine I have sustained him" (Gn 27:37).

The power of blessings and curses is also revealed in the amusing story of Balak and Balaam. Balak, King of Moab, summons Balaam, a non-Israelite prophet, in order to curse the people of Israel who have just finished their desert wanderings and are about to conquer the land of Canaan. "Come now, curse this people for me, since they are too mighty for me; perhaps I shall be able to defeat them and drive them from the land; for I know that he whom you bless is blessed, and he whom you curse is cursed" (Nm 22:6). Three times Balaam attempts to curse Israel, and on all three occasions blessings flow instead from his mouth. Of course, Balak is suitably infuriated, but he cannot refute Balaam's argument; "How can I curse whom God has not cursed? How can I denounce whom the Lord has not denounced?" (Nm 23:8). In fact, Balaam is only being intelligent—as Isaac's blessing said, anyone who curses Israel will be cursed themselves! Thus, Israel receives the lavish blessing of this pagan prophet summoned at the wish and expense of one of her enemies.

The power of speech is vividly conveyed in Proverbs and Psalms, where the tongue or the words that issue from it are often described in terms borrowed from the language of physical warfare. The tongue is seen as a weapon that can destroy an enemy as effectively as sword (Prv 12:18, 25:18; Ps 55:20-21, 64:3), spear (Ps 57:4), or arrow (Prv 25:18; Ps 57:4, 64:1-4). The tongue can be a war club (Prv 25:18), a scorching fire (Prv 16:27), or a sharp razor (Ps 52:1-4). One of the more lively images is found in Psalm 140:1-3:

> Deliver me, O Lord, from evil men;
>> preserve me from violent men,
> who plan evil things in their heart,
>> and stir up wars continually.
> They make their tongue sharp as a serpent's,
>> and under their lips is the poison of vipers.

All of this physical imagery is more than a poetic device. The ancient Israelites actually viewed words as having physical properties. And just as the world was created by a word and blessings were spoken and conveyed by a word, so could death and destruction be contained in a word. This is illustrated in the main set of laws in the Old Testament, the covenant code, found in Exodus 20-23. In Exodus 21:15 and 17 we have the following two laws drawn up in parallel form:

"Whoever strikes his father or his mother shall
be put to death."
"Whoever curses his father or his mother shall
be put to death."

Why the parallel form? It indicates clearly that to
curse someone damages them as much as a sharp
right to the jaw. Smiting and cursing are not just
metaphorically connected; they are each effective
means of assault that can cause serious damage to
another human being.

The ultimate force and power active in creation
is the word of God. Just as the world is created by
the power of God's word (Ps 33:4), so the natural
order is sustained by the same power:

fire and hail, snow and frost,
stormy wind fulfilling his command [lit.
"Word"] (Ps 148:8; see also Ps 147:15-20)

He reflects the glory of God and bears the very
stamp of his nature, upholding the universe by
his word of power. (Heb 1:3a)

Healing comes by the word of God:

Some were sick through their sinful ways,
and because of their iniquities suffered affliction;
they loathed any kind of food,
and they drew near to the gates of death.
Then they cried to the Lord in their trouble,
and he delivered them from their distress;

> he sent forth his word, and healed them,
> and delivered them from destruction.
> (Ps 107:17-20)

The word of God cuts through all human pretense
and reveals the true attitude of the heart:

> For the word of God is living and active,
> sharper than any two-edged sword, piercing to
> the division of soul and spirit, of joints and
> marrow, and discerning the thoughts and in-
> tentions of the heart. (Heb 4:12)

The word of God is the sword, wielded by
Christ and by his servants, which can overcome
any force attempting to resist it:

> Then I saw heaven opened, and behold, a white
> horse! He who sat upon it is called Faithful and
> True, and in righteousness he judges and makes
> war. His eyes are like a flame of fire, and on his
> head are many diadems; and he has a name
> inscribed which no one knows but himself. He
> is clad in a robe dipped in blood and the name
> by which he is called is The Word of God. And
> the armies of heaven, arrayed in fine linen,
> white and pure, followed him on white horses.
> *From his mouth issues a sharp sword with which to*
> *smite the nations,* and he will rule them with a
> rod of iron; he will tread the wine press of the
> fury of the wrath of God the Almighty.
> (Rv 19:11-15)

And take the helmet of salvation, and the sword of the Spirit, which is the word of God.

(Eph 6:17)

Finally, as shown in the passage from Revelation 19, Jesus himself is the word of God incarnate, the agent of creation, the one in whom all things hold together, the true revelation of the Almighty Father:

> In the beginning was the Word, and the Word was with God, and the Word was God. He was in the beginning with God; all things were made through him, and without him was not anything made that was made. In him was life, and the life was the light of men. . . .
> And the Word became flesh and dwelt among us, full of grace and truth. (Jn 1:1-4, 14a)

The power of the word is nowhere more evident than when looking at the word of *God*—the vital power that undergirds the created universe and brings salvation to those who will receive it.

The power of the word of God is vastly greater than the power of the word of man. Nonetheless, there is power in the word of man—a power deriving from the creation of the human race in the image and likeness of God. Human beings attain mastery through their words; their words have the power to heal or destroy (Prv 12:18), to give life or death (Prv 18:21). Speech can be a potent force for good or evil. This fact can help us understand why God is so concerned about the way we use our tongues.

Life and Death for Ourselves, Life and Death for Others

"Death and life are in the power of the tongue" (Prv 18:21). The biblical teaching is clear—our speech has tremendous potential for good or evil. The power of life and death that resides in our tongues applies both to our own lives and to the lives of others. Our words can lead *us* in the way of life or the way of death; they can also bring others along either of these paths.

God will hold us accountable for our words. They are thus a source of life or death for us. This is true in large part because our words reflect the condition of our heart. They serve as an external gauge for measuring the precise temperature of our internal heart disposition. Jesus teaches about this in Matthew 12:33-37:

> Either make the tree good, and its fruit good; or make the tree bad, and its fruit bad; for the tree is known by its fruit. You brood of vipers! how can you speak good, when you are evil? For out of the abundance of the heart the mouth speaks. The good man out of his good treasure brings forth good, and the evil man out of his evil treasure brings forth evil. I tell you, on the day of judgment men will render account for every

careless word they utter; for by your words you will be justified, and by your words you will be condemned.

I know of few verses in all of scripture more spine-chilling than the last two of this passage: "On the day of judgment men will render account for every careless word they utter; for by your words you will be justified, and by your words you will be condemned." However, these verses must be seen in their context. Careless words are a problem because they reflect a careless heart. "Out of the abundance of the heart the mouth speaks."

Derek Prince shares the following amusing and insightful anecdote in his book *Faith to Live By*:

As a hospital attendant with the British forces in North Africa during World War II, I worked for a while closely with a Scottish doctor in charge of a small field hospital that cared only for dysentery cases. Every morning as we went the round of our patients, the doctor invariably addressed each one with the same two sentences: "How are you? Show me your tongue!"

As I participated in this medical ritual each day, I observed that the doctor was much more interested in the state of the patient's tongue than in the answer that he received to the question, "How are you?" I have reflected many times since that the same is probably true of our relationship with God. We may offer

God our own estimate of our spiritual condition, but in the last resort God, like the doctor, judges mainly from our tongue.

An almost identical observation is made by a Christian teacher from quite a different era and tradition, Francis de Sales. In *Introduction to the Devout Life,* he writes:

> Physicians learn abut a man's health or sickness by looking at his tongue and our words are a true indication of the state of our souls. "By your words you will be justified and by your words you will be condemned," says the Savior.

If our hearts are right before the Lord—if they have been circumcised in Christ, renewed in the Holy Spirit, and surrendered fully to God in love and devotion—then our words will reflect our transformed condition and will be favorably received by our heavenly Father.

Our tongue does more than simply reflect the disposition of our heart; it also guides and orients our life in a particular direction. When we express a heart attitude with our lips—for example, faith and joy, or depression and discouragement—that attitude solidifies and tenaciously resists change. The words of our lips thus translate the thoughts of our hearts into patterns of behavior that harden into habits. Our lives are guided by what we think and what we say.

The letter of James emphasizes that mastery over our lives depends upon mastery over our tongues:

> For we all make many mistakes, and if any one makes no mistakes in what he says he is a perfect man, able to bridle the whole body also. If we put bits into the mouths of horses that they may obey us, we guide their whole bodies. Look at the ships also; though they are so great and are driven by strong winds, they are guided by a very small rudder wherever the will of the pilot directs. So the tongue is a little member and boasts great things. How great a forest is set ablaze by a small fire! (Jas 3:2-5)

Our tongue is like a bit that is put into the mouth of a horse—that one small piece of equipment will determine the movement of the entire animal. Similarly, our tongue is like the rudder of a ship— that one small piece of equipment will determine the movement of the entire vehicle. James thus teaches that the direction and orientation of our lives will depend on the direction and orientation of our tongues. Since the Lord attends closely to the words that issue from our mouth, we also should attend closely, if we desire to gain mastery over the rest of our lives and submit them fully to the authority of Christ.

However, the tongue is vital not only for ourselves; scripture insists even more strongly on the tongue's power to affect the lives of others around us. Righteous and unrighteous speech have consequences not only for the speaker, but also for those who hear and for those who are spoken about. Our words can build up, strengthen, and encourage others—they can impart life. Or our words can tear down, weaken, and dishearten others—they can cause death.

Paul tells us that our speech should benefit those who hear us: "Do not let any unwholesome talk come out of your mouths, but only what is helpful for building others up according to their needs, that it may benefit those who listen" (Eph 4:29 NIV). Our words can have a great positive impact on the lives of others. They can increase faith in God, secure hope in his promises, and build proper self-esteem. Scripture also teaches that our words can cause tremendous destruction: "A man who bears false witness against his neighbor is like a war club, or a sword, or a sharp arrow" (Prv 25:18, 11:9). With our speech we can rob someone of his good reputation, steal away his trust in others, and undermine faith, hope, and love. With our speech we can set brother against brother and sister against sister. Again the words of the sage apply: "Death and life are in the power of the tongue."

In the following pages I would like to explore the biblical teaching on the tongue in order to better understand how the Lord wants us to govern this spiritually "vital" organ. I want to focus especially on how our speech can bring life or death to other people. In the first few chapters

or death to other people. In the first few chapters
we will examine how our tongues can bring death
to others—our purpose, of course, being to avoid
this road. In the remaining chapters we will look at
how our speech can give life to others. Our aim is
to learn how to harness the explosive power of the
tongue that we might love the Lord with our
whole heart, soul, and strength, build up his body,
and give glory to his name.

TWO

Warring with the Tongue

SCRIPTURE TAKES verbal aggression as seriously as physical aggression. Consider this passage from the apocryphal/deuterocanonical book of Sirach:

> The blow of a whip raises a welt,
>   but a blow of the tongue crushes the bones.
> Many have fallen by the edge of the sword,
>   but not so many as have fallen because of the
>   tongue.
> Happy is the man who is protected from it,
>   who has not been exposed to its anger,
> Who has not borne its yoke,
>   and has not been bound with its fetters;
> for its yoke is a yoke of iron,
>   and its fetters are fetters of bronze;
> its death is an evil death,
>   and Hades is preferable to it. (Sir 28:17-21)

Sirach clearly states the point also made in Proverbs and Psalms: not only is verbal aggression as serious and dangerous as physical aggression, but at times it is even more lethal and more to be dreaded. Just as scripture teaches us much about physical aggression, so it also teaches us about verbal aggression.

Verbal aggression is all speech used with the intent of harming another. Scripture teaches about five main types of verbal aggression:

1. *Cursing.* Calling upon a supernatural power to bring harm on another (Ex 21:17, 22:28; Lv 19:14).

2. *Reviling.* Insulting and hurling verbal abuse at another (Ex 22:28; 1 Cor 5:11, 6:9-10).

3. *Guile.* Using deceitful and misleading words to cloak malicious intentions (Ps 10:7, 52:1-4, 101:5, 7; Rom 1:29-31; 1 Pt 2:1, 2:22-23, 3:9-10).

4. *False Witness.* Testifying falsely in a court of law to another's harm (Ex 20:16; Prv 19:5, 9, 25:18).

5. *Slander.* Speaking evil of another, usually to third parties (Ex 23:1-3; Lv 19:16; Nm 12:1-3, 8; Jas 4:11-12; 1 Pt 2:1).

These are all ways of using our speech to damage another's reputation, break their confidence, and even cause them material loss. Each act of verbal aggression ruptures personal relationships and leads to mistrust, malice, and resentment.

Of these five forms of tongue warfare, the last one—slander—is of special importance, at least for most of us. Cursing, reviling, guile, and false witness are all easy for us to detect in ourselves. They are like bulky cannons rolled out for the big kill. Slander, on the other hand, is far more subtle, more often undetected, and much more common among Christians. It is a weapon that many of us wield deftly and lethally without even consciously recognizing that we are drawing blood. Therefore, we will devote the present chapter to slander— what it is, what scripture teaches about it, and what we should do about it.

Slander/Speaking Against

The English word "slander" is most often used to translate a cluster of Hebrew and Greek words in scripture that all relate to a particular pattern of sinful speech. However, the English word "slander" is not really an adequate translation of these terms. The dictionary defines it as "the utterance of false charges or misrepresentations which defame and damage another's reputation." A person who slanders in the modern English sense issues charges and accusations that contradict the true facts of the case—the charges are false and distorted. In contrast, the biblical words focus less on the truth or falsehood underlying the charges made and more on the inappropriateness of making them in the first place.

One of the Greek words used in the New Testament to express this concept can be literally translated as "speaking against" (*katalalous*). The word means to make personal accusations and charges that one has no authority to make. The word does not imply that the charges are false— only that one does not have the right to make them. This understanding of "slander" is also echoed clearly in the *Shulchan Aruch,* an authoritative compendium of Jewish law from the sixteenth century:

> There is a much graver sin than talebearing, and this is slander, that is, when a man talks disparagingly about someone, *although he is telling the truth.* If one maliciously invents untruths about a person, he is guilty of defamation of character as well. A slanderer is one who says: "So and so has done such and such a thing; so and so were his parents; such and such a thing have I heard about him"; and the nature of the thing tends to disgrace him. . . . The decree of annihilation against our forefathers in the wilderness was sealed only on account of their tendency to slander.

According to this definition, "slander" occurs especially when the facts summoned are accurate. It is a sin because the facts are summoned for the purpose of dishonoring and disgracing an individual. This understanding of "slander" is closer to the biblical notion than is the modern understanding.

We can look to the book of James for one of

the clearest New Testament passages prohibiting slander/speaking against:

> Do not speak against one another, brethren. He who speaks against a brother, or judges his brother, speaks against the law, and judges the law; but if you judge the law, you are not a doer of the law, but a judge of it. There is only one Lawgiver and Judge, the One who is able to save and to destroy; but who are you who judge your neighbor? (4:11-12 NAS)

The "law" that James speaks of here is probably the second great commandment, "You shall love your neighbor as yourself," which he refers to earlier (2:8). "To judge" here means to judge unfavorably, to condemn; it is synonymous with "speaking against." To speak against a brother is thus to assume a position of authority over him, a position in which one has the right to evaluate and render an authoritative verdict on his conduct. To judge is to investigate facts, weigh evidence, hear charges, render a verdict, and pronounce a sentence. When we take this position in relation to a brother when God has not give us the authority to do so, then we find ourselves also speaking against and judging and condemning the law of God which commands us to love our brothers; we thus find ourselves in the precarious position of judging and speaking against God, who instituted this law.

This passage in James, along with Jesus' words

against judging others in Matthew 7:1-2 (which James appears to be commenting on), must be viewed with other New Testament passages that speak of a proper type of judgment that should be found within the church. For example, Paul writes:

> Do you not know that the saints will judge the world? And if the world is to be judged by you, are you incompetent to try trivial cases? Do you not know that we are to judge angels? How much more, matters pertaining to this life!
>
> (1 Cor 6:2-3)

There are situations where God gives us the authority to act as a judge—to investigate facts, weigh evidence, hear charges, render a verdict, and even pronounce a sentence. A parent acts as a judge in a family every time he or she tries to sort out a squabble among the children. An elder in a Christian community is supposed to act as a judge in many situations. When God gives us the authority to act as a judge, we must act with grace, love, and concern for others, but also with strength and firmness. But when God has not given us this authority, then we must not act as though he has. This is the heart of James' message to us.

In the many passages in the New Testament that forbid us to slander or speak against others, three Greek words are often translated by the English word "slander." However, the words have slightly different meanings, and these nuances can help us understand how serious slander is. The first word, *katalalos,* is used in James 4:11-12, and, as noted earlier, can be literally translated as "speaking against." Other New Testament prohibitions of slander which use this word can be found in Romans 1:30, 2 Corinthians 12:20, and 1 Peter 2:1. The second Greek word often translated as slander is *diabolos* (literally, "slanderer"), the word often used in the New Testament to refer to Satan. The English word "devil" is derived from this term. The intimate identification of slander with the Evil One demonstrates clearly the New Testament revulsion in the face of this type of wrongdoing. The word is used in 1 Timothy 3:11, 2 Timothy 3:3, and Titus 2:3 to refer to slander on the purely human level. The third word for slander is *blasphemia,* another word that has been transferred into the English language, though with some change in meaning. The English word "blasphemy" denotes an act of sacrilege, an act of speaking against God or against that which is closely associated with him. In New Testament Greek, however, the word simply means to speak badly of someone, be it God, man, or angel. There are many instances in the New Testament where it clearly refers to speaking against human beings and is condemned accordingly (see Mt 15:19; Eph 4:31; Col 3:8, 1 Tm 6:4; 2 Tm 3:2). A passage from Titus is especially clear:

Remind them to be submissive to rulers and authorities, to be obedient, to be ready for any honest work, *to speak evil* of no one, to avoid quarrelling, to be gentle, and to show perfect courtesy toward all men. (3:1-2)

Whether the word be *katalalos, diabolos,* or *blasphemia,* the meaning is essentially the same: we are forbidden by scripture to speak of one another in a way that destroys another's reputation or questions his basic righteousness or competence, except in a very few specific and limited situations.

There may be some teachings in scripture whose purpose is hidden from us and which we obey simply because God ordained them, but the prohibition of slander/speaking against is not among them. The practice of speaking against others destroys trust and undermines committed personal relationships. I had an opportunity to reflect on this fact recently as I conversed with an old friend. He lived in another city and participated in the leadership of a religious organization there. As he described the inner workings of the group, he made it clear who were the good guys and who were the bad guys. I was not conscious of the fact at the time, but my opinions about those people he described were being formed by the information and perspectives he passed on to me. If I were to meet any of those "bad guys" today, I would distrust them immediately. My opinions were set before having any immediate personal contact with the individuals concerned. I had no way to verify my friend's observations, but my mind had already absorbed them. My friend had no reason or authority to speak to me of these internal affairs, and I had no right to hear them. This is the way that slander works—it catches us off guard and plants in us an orientation of suspicion, criticalness, and mistrust.

In Jewish tradition the great biblical example of slander is the incident of Miriam and Aaron speaking against Moses:

> Miriam and Aaron spoke against Moses because of the Cushite woman whom he had married, for he had married a Cushite woman; and they said, "Has the Lord indeed spoken only through Moses? Has he not spoken through us also?" And the Lord heard it. (Nm 12:1-2)

We must remember that Moses is the brother of Miriam and Aaron. We therefore find two causes of slander in this passage, two causes that are just as common today as they must have been in ancient Israel. First, we have a family dispute. "Look at the woman he married! She's a foreigner, a stranger, she's not one of our people. She's never really learned to speak Hebrew well—have you heard how she rolls her r's? And with all of this going against her, she has the nerve to act as though she's superior to us! And just because she's the wife of *Moses*!" The family dispute then shifts into a complaint against authority. "I do think Moses has been getting a bit uppity as of late. All of that time on the mountain must be getting to him. He's beginning to act like he's the sole oracle of God, the only leader in Israel! Now don't get me wrong—I admit that Moses did an OK job of getting us out of Egypt. But remember, Aaron is the eloquent one, the one who can really handle himself before a group of people. He was Moses' spokesman in Egypt, and is now the High Priest of Israel. And Miriam has always been a fine prophetic leader—do you remember her marvelous dance by the Red Sea? So why is Moses the one who always gives the orders?" As the passage says, the Lord heard the complaining words of Miriam and Aaron. As a father deals with bickering children, the Lord now calls them forward and deals with them:

And suddenly the Lord said to Moses and to Aaron and Miriam, "Come out, you three, to the tent of meeting." And the three of them came out. And the Lord came down in a pillar of cloud, and stood at the door of the tent, and called Aaron and Miriam; and they both came forward. And he said, "Hear my words: If there is a prophet among you, I the Lord make myself known to him in a vision, I speak with him in a dream. Not so with my servant Moses; he is entrusted with all my house. With him I speak mouth to mouth, clearly, and not in dark speech; and he beholds the form of the Lord. *Why then were you not afraid to speak against my servant Moses?*" (Nm 12:4-8)

The Lord then punishes Miriam with a temporary case of leprosy—a disease that indicated her state of uncleanness before the Lord (we judge from the punishment that she was the main instigator behind the sin). This passage helps explain the Jewish view expressed in the earlier quote from *Shulchan Aruch*: "The decree of annihilation against our forefathers in the wilderness was sealed only on account of their tendency to slander."

The two causes of slander in Numbers 12 also operate among us. Many of us yield to the impulse to speak against members of our family or against in-laws. We have resentments that have accumulated over the years and find release through our mouths—though in fact speaking out of resentment does not release it but only increases it. Many of us also yield to the urge to complain about our boss or our pastor. This speech pattern builds mistrust for the person in authority and makes it all the more difficult for him to exercise his authority and for others to submit themselves to it. We may not be punished with leprosy when we speak in these ways, but we may be sure that God is not pleased with us.

Scripture takes slander/speaking against very seriously. It would certainly endorse the following words of Francis de Sales:

Rash judgment begets uneasiness, contempt of neighbor, pride, self-satisfaction, and many other extremely bad effects. Slander, the true plague of society, holds first place among them. I wish that I had a burning coal taken from the holy altar to purify men's lips so that their iniquities might be removed and their sins washed away, as did the seraphim who purified Isaiah's mouth. The man who could free the world of slander would free it of a large share of its sins and iniquity.

Slander is one of the most common and deadly forms of verbal aggression found in our society today, and it is one from which Christians are not immune. If we could root out slander from our families, work sites, and churches, our relationships with others would improve dramatically and our lives would conform more closely to God's plan.

The Alternative

Several months ago, I told a relative about the biblical teaching on slander. His reaction was instructive: "If we can't speak about others' evil doing and incompetence, what *are* we supposed to do? Bury our heads in the sand and pretend that everyone we know is beautiful and holy? Are we supposed to let wickedness go unchecked and error go unchallenged? What is the alternative to speaking against others when they are actually in the wrong?" The question could be formulated in this way: If slander is the wrong response to the sin and incompetence of others, what is the right response?

The proper response among Christians is set forth clearly in Matthew 18:15-17:

> And if your brother sins, go and reprove him in private; if he listens to you, you have won your brother. But if he does not listen to you, take one or two more with you, so that by the mouth of two or three witnesses every fact may be confirmed [Dt 19:15]. And if he refuses to listen to them, tell it to the church; and if he refuses to listen even to the church, let him be to you as a Gentile and a tax-gatherer. (NAS)

If I have seen my brother do something wrong, then I am to go directly to him and discuss the matter with him "in private." I am not to broadcast the facts as I saw them to my neighbors, friends, relatives, co-workers, and fellow church members, but instead I am to confront the person himself, talk over the situation with him, and try to help him deal righteously with what he has done.

Unfortunately, many of us are ready to talk with everyone about our brother's sins and faults except with the brother himself. It is much easier to complain and criticize to third parties than it is to go directly to a brother and point out his fault. We are afraid to talk *with* the brother himself, but we are not afraid to talk *about* him. Yet genuine Christian love should compel us to do whatever we

can to help a brother improve, change, and grow,
or even be restored to full fellowship with God:

> My brethren, if any one among you wanders
> from the truth and some one brings him back,
> let him know that whoever brings back a sinner
> from the error of his way will save his soul from
> death and will cover a multitude of sins.
>
> (Jas 5:19-20)

The words of Christ are just as clear: "If your
brother sins, go and reprove him in private; if he
listens to you, you have won your brother" (Mt
18:15 NAS). Our aim should be to win our brother
rather than to lose him.

This aim will be reflected in the way we go to
our brother. We should not reprove our brother
arrogantly, aggressively, challenging and provoking him to react defensively and in anger. Paul
teaches us how to administer the reproof: "Brethren, if a man is overtaken in any trespass, you who
are spiritual should restore him in a spirit of
gentleness" (Gal 6:1). We should be courteous
and considerate, expressing genuine concern for
the brother. We should also be eager to find out
that our perception of the facts is inaccurate.
Nonetheless, we must present our concern to the
brother firmly, clearly, and without ambiguity.
The more concrete and specific we can be, the
better. For example, it is better not to correct a
brother for "pride" and "selfishness," which are

general qualities that are open to subjective interpretation, and better to correct him for how he
actually mishandled this particular situation. The
more specific and concrete the correction, the
easier it is to respond to receptively and with zeal
to change. Our aim throughout should be to win
our brother, not to criticize and attack him.

In addition to going to the brother himself with
a reproof or a concern, it is also possible to go to an
appropriate authority who has some responsibility
for the brother. This is what Jesus means when he
says, "tell it to the church." The word "church"
here probably refers to the elders of the community who are able to represent the body in such
juridical matters. According to the words of
Jesus, we should begin by going to the brother
personally and in private, and only bring the
matter before the church when other more direct
methods have proved ineffective. The most direct
approach is clearly preferred. However, there are
occasions when it is necessary and helpful to go to
the appropriate authority, even before confronting
the brother directly. For example, if you have
reason to believe that a direct confrontation could
irreparably damage your relationship with the
brother, or if you are persuaded that the brother
would not be able to receive the reproof from you,
then it might be best to go immediately to
someone responsible for the person who could
assist in administering the correction. Even so,
one only resorts to an outside authority when one

is convinced that a more direct method of correction will prove ineffective and perhaps even detrimental.

There are many possible authorities that can be helpful in resolving questions of wrongdoing or incompetence. If one is dealing with a young person, then it may be best to present the concern before the young man's or woman's father. In matters internal to the life of the Christian community, it is also possible to approach the person's pastor and to enlist his help. There may even be situations where it is appropriate to go to one's boss with a concern about a fellow-worker. Whenever there is a clear line of authority and personal responsibility in the situation, it is possible to seek help from someone else in correcting a brother.

If we are going to seek help from an appropriate authority in dealing with a brother's wrong, we must be willing to be identified to the brother. We should not cling to anonymity. Going to an authority is not a way of shirking our responsibility and getting someone else to do the dirty work. Rather, its purpose is to render correction more effective. If you bring a concern about a brother to a pastor, that pastor must be free to say to the brother that it was you who raised the concern. It is unfair for the brother to be questioned about wrongdoing or incompetence without knowing who first raised the question. The secular legal system has long recognized that it is wrong to try a defendant without ever allowing him to face directly his accuser or the witnesses for the prosecution. Christians should be just as careful; if we love our brother and want to help the proper authority uncover the full truth, we must put aside our anonymity and allow ourselves to be identified as the source of the information.

The only people we should talk to about a brother's sin are the brother himself and an appropriate authority. If we cannot go directly to the person and we also cannot take the matter to an appropriate authority, then we must learn to live with it. We are not free to talk about it at will. To talk to others about someone's sin is slander.

There are a couple of exceptions to this rule. First of all, if we cannot talk to the individual or to an authority about the person's sin, and if this poses a major personal difficulty for us, we can seek advice about what to do from a wise and experienced brother or sister. This must be done carefully and, if possible, without revealing the identity of the person whose wrongdoing we are discussing. Secondly, we occasionally may need to warn others about someone based on information at our disposal. For example, perhaps we have reliable knowledge that teenage Sally down the block likes to steal things when she babysits. In addition to dealing directly with Sally and her parents (and perhaps the police), we may want to warn people not to hire Sally as a babysitter. We thereby protect others from Sally and perhaps protect Sally from herself.

The New Testament teaching on slander and correction is directed mainly to Christians in their relationships with one another ("If your *brother* sins," Mt 18:15). Nevertheless, the same fundamental principles apply to relationships outside the Christian community. When a Christian sees the sin of a non-Christian neighbor or business associate, he does not have the right to speak of it indiscriminately to his Christian friends. He must either go to the person himself, to some authority who has concern for him, or else forbear. We are not free to level accusations and charges against someone just because they lack a Christian commitment.

Unfortunately, forbearance is easier to talk about than to practice. This is true for relationships with both Christians and non-Christians. The other guy's insolence, or stupidity, or incompetence, or thoughtlessness grates and grinds on us, and our fleshly response is to lash out in a complaint. If we know that slander is wrong we may formulate our complaint in a subtle and indirect fashion, communicating our displeasure and judgment with hints, gestures, and frowns, rather than with an explicit accusation. However, our complaint has been registered. The biblical teaching, on the other hand, calls us to a different approach. If we decide to forbear a person's mistake or sin rather than confront them with it personally or bring it to a proper authority, then we should drop the matter and not pick it up again. It may be difficult; the sinful flesh may rebel; still, anything less is not true Christian forbearance.

The real alternative to slander is courtesy and the showing of honor. I have found a simple rule very helpful in guarding my tongue against slander: Everything I say about a person should increase the esteem my listeners have for that person. If I am saying something that will in any way lower others' esteem for him, then I probably should not be saying it. Many times my mouth has been shut in mid-sentence when I remember this simple rule. It would not be so difficult to avoid slander if we developed better habits of showing honor and commendation with our tongue.

Shut Your Ears

The Bible not only forbids us to speak slander; it also teaches us to refuse to listen to the slander of others. Slander is not a solitary sin; it takes at least two to slander—one to speak, and one to listen. It is like a forward pass in the game of football: your quarterback may have a terrific arm, but if his receivers refuse to catch the ball his pass will not be successful. If no one ever listened to slander, all slanderers would probably grow discouraged and retire from the game.

Most of us probably think of listening as a mere passive event for which we bear no responsibility. The person who speaks must take responsibility for what he says; our part is simply to listen and decide what we think. However, this is not the perspective found in scripture:

> An evildoer listens to wicked lips;
> and a liar gives heed to a mischievous tongue.
> (Prv 17:4)

According to this proverb, the type of things we listen to reveal the type of person we are. A liar listens to lies, a mischievous person listens to mischief, a slanderer listens to slander. This is analogous to the New Testament teaching which asserts that what we say reveals who we are. We bear responsibility both for what we say and what we hear, and they will both reflect the type of person we really are.

We can actively shut our ears to slander in two ways. First, we can avoid the company of those who regularly speak slander, or at least refuse to discuss issues that might lead to slander. A passage from Sirach is instructive here:

> Do not argue about a matter which does not
> concern you,
> nor sit with sinners when they judge a case.
> (11:9)

We should refuse to be drawn into discussions that involve people and events and possible wrongs that are outside of our sphere of responsibility and concern. We should also reject the subtle invitations to join a self-appointed private court that is holding a trial in the absence of the defendant. We always have a choice in these matters. We can either allow ourselves to be drawn into these situations or we can avoid them. The righteous man or woman will avoid them like the plague—or, more appropriately, like leprosy.

We cannot always avoid the company of those who produce slander. We may need to associate with them at our place of employment, or they may be our relatives, or they may be people the Lord is calling us to influence positively. However, we can refuse to listen to their slander. As soon as they begin to make accusations and charges, we can show our disinterest and even our displeasure. We need not defend the people accused—this will often only draw out further accusations. But we can explain that we are not interested in hearing negative talk about people for whom we bear no responsibility and whom we have no authority to judge.

The second way that we can shut our ears to slander is to refuse to take heed of the slanderous information that has been passed on to us. Another passage from Sirach elaborates on this point:

Question a friend, perhaps he did not do it;
    but if he did anything, so that he may do it no
      more.
Question a neighbor, perhaps he did not say it;
    but if he said it, so that he may not say it
      again.
Question a friend, for often it is slander;
    so do not believe everything you hear.

> A person may make a slip without intending it.
> Who has never sinned with his tongue?
>   (Sir 19:13-16)

When we hear charges and accusations, do we immediately give credence to what we have heard? Our usual reaction to slander is to trust the person speaking to us and to mistrust the person being spoken against. Sirach cautions us against such a response: "Do not believe everything your hear." Sirach would have us exchange the parties of our trust—we should instinctively mistrust a slanderer and immediately give the benefit of the doubt to the object of his charges. We are also urged to go to the person himself and verify the accusations—we will either clear a friend of suspicion or perhaps help him to fall no more. Telling a slanderer that you are going directly to the person accused of wrong is also a good way to shut up a slanderer. A slanderer usually prefers to "lie in ambush" with his tongue (Sir 5:14) rather than face his opponent in an open duel.

Bill Gothard draws a helpful analogy between slander and a communicable disease. A slanderer is a body carrying an infection, and our exposure to him and his accusations puts us in risk of being similarly contaminated. If we allow ourselves to hear his complaints and charges, then his deadly bacteria are communicated to us. We are infected by these germs as they overcome our normal defense systems, and our body becomes diseased as our vital life-supporting functions are attacked.

According to this analogy, the critical step is to avoid contamination in the first place—to refuse to listen to slander. But once we have heard the charges we must take special precautions to see that our normal defenses are not overcome by the alien bacteria. In other words, we must refuse to believe what we have heard and fight actively against the temptation to be mistrustful or suspicious of the accused party. If we are careful, we can still avoid the disease. This analogy points out vividly the importance of neither listening to nor heeding slander.

Gothard calls slander "an evil report." He gives some excellent advice on how to detect a carrier of an evil report and how to detect an evil report. They are as follows:

How to Detect a Carrier of an Evil Report

A. A carrier will usually *test your spirit* before giving you the evil report. Any evidence of a compatible spirit in you will encourage him to give you the report.

B. A carrier will usually *check your acceptance* of his report before giving it to you. He may do this by asking for your opinion about the person or dropping a negative comment and observing your response to it.

C. A carrier will often *get you to ask* for the evil report by creating curiosity for it. Some starters are "Have you heard about (the person)?" "Wait 'til I tell you about (the person)!"

D. A carrier may communicate an evil report by *asking you for counsel* or by sharing a concern for the person involved.

E. A carrier may use evil reports to *get you to admire* him or her for being on the inside and having access to privileged information.

F. A carrier is usually one who *evokes vivid details* of evil and will even search them out. God condemns such "detectives of darkness" whose tongues are like sharp swords.

How to Detect an Evil Report:

Five questions to ask *before* listening to a carrier:

A. "What is your reason for telling me?"
Widening the circle of gossip only compounds the problem.

B. "Where did you get your information?"
Refusal to identify the source of information is a sure signal of an evil report.

C. "Have you gone to those directly involved?"
Spirituality is not measured by how well we expose an offender, but by how effectively we restore an offender (Gal 6:1).

D. "Have you personally checked out all of the facts?"
Even "facts" become distorted when not balanced with other facts or when given with negative motives.

E. "Can I quote you if I check this out?"
Those who give evil reports often claim that
they are "misquoted." This is because their
words and overriding impressions are reported.

If we apply each of these tests and ask each of these
questions, we will be quick to detect slander and
better able to avoid its contamination.

It is often difficult to decide to not listen to
slander. Accusations and charges fascinate our
fallen flesh; curiosity, desire to be "in the know,"
pleasure in the sensational and unusual, mixed
together with baser motives of malice, envy, and
spite, make us an easy catch for the tempter. This
is perhaps the meaning of Proverbs 18:8a: "The
words of a whisperer are like delicious morsels."
However, the results of eating these morsels are
not at all pleasant. First of all, as stated in Proverbs
18:8b, "they go down into the inner parts of the
body." Slander eats away at us from the depths of
our being, coloring our thoughts, feelings, and
attitudes with criticalness, suspicion, mistrust,
and contempt. Secondly, we open ourselves up to
a steady diet of the same poison. As Proverbs 29:12
puts it, "If a ruler listens to falsehood, all his
officials will be wicked." If a king is willing to
listen to wicked counsel, then he will quickly have
a court filled with evil counsellors. Similarly, if we
begin showing a receptivity to slanderous charges,
we are destined to hear them repeatedly. A
slanderer knows when he owns someone's ear.
Thirdly, listening to slander drives away all peace

and contentment. Sirach contributes this insight:
"Whoever pays heed to slander will not find rest,
nor will he settle down in peace" (28:16). Slander
destroys personal relationships and leads to a
fearful and insecure existence—for the slanderer,
those who hear it, and those who are its object.
Therefore, regardless how strong the temptation
to listen to slander, we will all find ourselves in
better health if this "delicious morsel" is never
eaten, in fact, if it is never served.

THREE

Whispering with a Neighbor

OPEN VERBAL AGRESSION—such as slander—is not the only way that we can damage people with our tongues. There is another even more subtle speech pattern that undermines trust and soils a reputation: gossip. Gossip always involves talking about people in a manner that is in some way harmful. It does not produce outright charges of wrongdoing or incompetence, but it spins a web of innuendo and information that binds a person's name and subjects it to criticism and dishonor. We gossip whenever we talk about people in a manner that will diminish our hearers' trust and esteem for them, and whenever we reveal another's personal thoughts and affairs without their permission. Gossip is another important means by which the tongue's power to destroy is manifested.

Biblical Teaching

We may think of gossip as a petty sin, an almost laughable and easily forgivable violation of the divine order. However, scripture takes gossip seriously. For example, Paul includes gossip in a bloodcurdling list of sins that derive from the human race's refusal to worship and honor God the Creator:

> And since they did not see fit to acknowledge God, God gave them up to a base mind and to improper conduct. They were filled with all manner of wickedness, evil, covetousness, malice. Full of envy, murder, strife, deceit, malignity, they are *gossips,* slanderers, haters of God, insolent, haughty, boastful, inventors of evil, disobedient to parents, foolish, faithless, heartless, ruthless. (Rom 1:28-31)

We can also learn about gossip from the company it keeps in 2 Corinthians 12:20, where it is surrounded again by words that denote serious sin in personal relationships:

> For I fear that perhaps I may come and find you not what I wish, and that you may find me not what you wish; that perhaps there may be quarrelling, jealousy, anger, selfishness, slander, *gossip,* conceit, and disorder.

The Greek word in these passages (*psithurismos*) literally means "whispering" (the word, like its English counterpart, sounds like the reality it stands for). It suggests critical innuendo and the underhanded revealing of secrets. The apostle Paul condemns *psithurismos* with force and without qualification.

Paul uses another term for gossip in 1 Timothy 5:13. He is giving his rationale for why young widows should remarry, relating his personal experience of what often happens when they remain unattached:

> Besides that, they learn to be idlers, gadding about from house to house, and not only idlers but *gossips* and busybodies, saying what they should not.

The Greek word used here refers to silly and useless speech, foolish communication about serious or private matters, talk that has no constructive purpose yet flows on like a powerful cataract. It derives from a Greek word that means "to boil over" or "overflow." Once again, we see that the apostle has no room for gossip among his recommended qualities of Christian character; those who gossip are "saying what they should not."

The book of Proverbs singles out one particular feature of gossip as especially worthy of reproach: the revealing of secrets.

> He who belittles his neighbor lacks sense,
>   but a man of understanding remains silent.
> He who goes about as a talebearer reveals secrets,
>   but he who is trustworthy in spirit keeps a thing hidden. (11:12-13)

> He who goes about gossiping reveals secrets;
> therefore do not associate with one who
> speaks foolishly. (20:19)

When you disseminate personal and private information, you prove yourself untrustworthy and disloyal. This is particularly true if you possess the information because a friend confided in you. In scripture one of the surest tokens of friendship is openness about one's true intentions, thoughts, and concerns. "No longer do I call you servants, for the servant does not know what his master is doing; but I have called you friends, for all that I have heard from my Father I have made known to you" (Jn 15:15). This is the reason why Abraham is called the friend of God (Is 41:8): "The Lord said, 'Shall I hide from Abraham what I am about to do?'" (Gn 18:17). To treat lightly information that is received as a result of a privileged relationship is to abuse one's comrade and show oneself unworthy of friendship. The unfaithfulness is especially gross if the revelations tend to belittle the one who put his trust in you. Gossip thus violates friendship by broadcasting openly what was confided in a few trusted ears.

We find much helpful commentary on these proverbs in the book of Sirach:

> One who rejoices in wickedness will be condemned,
>   and for one who hates gossip evil is lessened.
> Never repeat a conversation,

and you will lose nothing at all.
With friend or foe do not report it,
  and unless it would be a sin for you, do not
  disclose it. (19:5-8)

To the basic exhortation not to repeat personal
conversations, Sirach adds one important qualification: If for some reason righteousness demands
that we reveal something confided in us, then we
must follow the higher law. If we are privy to a
murder plot, we are not obliged to keep it secret in
loyalty to our friends.

Have you heard a word? Let it die with you.
  Be brave! It will not make you burst!
With such a word a fool will suffer pangs
  like a woman in labor with a child.
Like an arrow stuck in the flesh of the thigh,
  so is a word inside a fool. (19:10-12)

These are certainly among the most memorable
and amusing lines in the book of Sirach. In a few
brief and vivid images the author ridicules the
seemingly irrespressible urge of the gossip to
reveal hidden information. The effort required for
the gossip to hold his tongue is portrayed as
heroic. Yet he is given a grain of encouragement:
the effort will not prove fatal!

Whoever betrays secrets destroys confidence,
  and he will never find a congenial friend.
Love your friend and keep faith with him;

but if you betray his secrets, do not run after
    him.
For as a man destroys his enemy,
    so you have destroyed the friendship of your
        neighbor. (27:16-18)

The gossip thus does damage not only to the
offended party, but also to himself. He destroys
the relationships he already has, and ensures that
he will find no congenial friends in the future.
Who wants to confide in one who has proven that
he cannot keep faith? The gossip therefore ends up
lonely, isolated, friendless.

According to Sirach, Proverbs, and the apostle
Paul, gossip is no light matter. It is a source of bad
relationships, and it is seriously displeasing to
God. One who desires to live in righteousness will
flee from gossip like a deer before a hunter.

Pitfalls and Paths

We now need to translate these biblical principles and directives into the practical language of
our daily lives. Over the years I have noted four
major pitfalls which cause many of us to tumble
into gossip. They are four ways of talking about
other people that inevitably lead us into "saying
what we should not" (1 Tm 5:13).

*1. Speaking about other people's problems in a
way that could reflect on their character or competence.* Everyone faces objective challenges, difficulties, and problems in their lives. Your mother

dies, your car gets smashed while it is sitting in a parking lot minding its own business, you lose your job because your plant closes down. Problems like these do not reflect on one's character or competence, and it is therefore not necessarily wrong for others to speak about them. However, there are certain problems and certain ways of talking about them that tend to smear a person's reputation. The following examples make the point: "I hear John was fired from his job last week." "Did you know that Fred and Sally are having marital problems?" "Have you heard that Carl's son has a drinking problem?" "Ruth sure seems to get into a lot of automobile accidents." Though no explicit accusations are levelled in any of these comments, it is not difficult to draw out the implications.

2. *Speaking about other people's weaknesses, temptations, and sins.* We may know about others' weaknesses, temptations, or sins because they have talked with us about them or because we have been present while they were manifested in action. Either way, we should not speak of these things unless we have received explicit permission to do so or we feel obliged to seek out help for them. It is a serious breach of faith to share such things as the following: "Did you know that Sarah has to fight daily against her old alcohol problem?" "I hear that Jim has a strong attraction to pornography." "Though she hates herself for it, Dorothy will often fly into a rage and beat the kids silly." "Al puts on a good front, but internally I've heard he's

quite emotionally unstable." "Put Chuck in the wrong environment, and he'll gamble away his car, his house, his wife and children." Talk like this helps no one.

3. *Speaking about other people's private and personal affairs.* Many things in people's lives should remain discreetly hidden unless they choose to divulge them. We are free to reveal details of our own lives, but not the details of others. The sorts of things I have in mind are not necessarily negative or scandalous; they are simply not intended to be paraded before the public eye. Examples are comments like this: "I hear that John and Mary don't use any birth control." "Sam told me that he really dislikes his new boss." "Who is Carol dating now?" "Charles made seventy-five thousand dollars last year." A friend may share these things with you about himself, but you are not then free to pass them on to others.

4. *Speaking critically about various areas of other people's lives.* This way of speaking involves our rendering an opinion on some feature of another's life when we have no authority or sound reason to do so. I am not thinking here of charges of major wrongdoing or incompetence—that would move us from the realm of gossip into the realm of slander. Instead, the criticisms issued in gossip are often small and in apparently trivial matters. Yet they are barbed and they leave a wound. The following are examples of such criticisms: "I think Nancy has such poor taste in clothing." "If you ask me, Tom and Laura don't spank their children

often enough." "I wish Dave would re-paint that ugly garage of his." "It's a wonder Laura ever passed her driver's test—she's awful behind the wheel." As with slander, the proper ones to hear our complaints and criticisms are the people who are the objects of them or some other proper authority. To pass such comments along to others is pure and undiluted gossip.

It may seem as though these four pitfalls rule out *all* talking about other people, but this is not the case. There are many ways of speaking about people that are permissible and even helpful. For example, it is good to speak of other people's virtues and admirable qualities: "Jean is a wonderful seamstress—and so generous in helping others with their sewing." "Gary is a very devoted and faithful father." It is also good to speak of others' successes: "I hear that Fred was the most productive salesman at his branch this past year." "Ellen finished painting the portrait just in time for Art's birthday, and Art loved it." We can also pass on freely the blessings others have experienced: "Martha had a beautiful baby." "Roger is recovering very well from his illness." "Bill and Jeanne's eldest son just committed his life to the Lord." Sometimes the English word "gossip" is used to refer to all speaking about other peoples' lives, including the positive comments that I just described. Though there is a danger of talking too much about other people, there is also a danger in talking too much about football or cars or literature. Any topic (other than the Lord himself) that dominates our speech can become a problem, but this is not the biblical meaning of the word "gossip." Gossip means useless, silly, and critical speech about other people, speech that subtracts from the respect and esteem your listeners have for them.

When you and a friend are discussing someone with whom you both have a relationship, it may also be appropriate to pass on some more neutral information that can help you to keep up with one another's lives. This type of information is often simply on the order of "news": "I hear that Jim has started a new job." "Sam and Alice bought a new car last week." "The Browns will be away on vacation for two weeks." Once again, there is a danger in getting preoccupied with the communication of such facts—they can feed a problem we may have with idle curiosity. Nonetheless, there is nothing intrinsically wrong with sharing this type of neutral information, and sometimes it is necessary and helpful.

As stated earlier, it is even appropriate at times to talk with friends about other people's objective challenges and problems. This is especially the case when there is some way that we can help them respond to the problem. "Did you hear that Marge's mother had a serious car accident yesterday? Perhaps we could take care of her kids for a few days and free her to deal properly with the situation." "Ralph has been laid flat again by his bad back. How about if we visit him, and maybe do a little bit of work around his house?" Sometimes it is helpful to share such things simply in order to enlist prayer support. However, we must be especially careful that we not talk about problems in a way that might denigrate or dishonor those we are speaking of.

Sometimes situations may arise where we feel obligated to talk about someone else's weaknesses, temptations, or sins with a person who might be able to help them. Ordinarily we should not do this without first consulting the individual with the difficulty and gaining their approval. However, there may be cases where it is appropriate to go to one's pastor or a close friend who can take the initiative in helping the troubled person. For example, I have a friend who is an experienced drug-abuse counsellor. Sometimes people tell him about their friends' or relatives' troubles and ask for advice or for active assistance. Such communication can be a way of serving another person, although we must be careful not to use this as an excuse for gossip.

As with slander, we are just as guilty in listening to gossip as we are in speaking it. I might add that we are also just as guilty in reading gossip as we are in listening to it. Dozens of publications thrive on purveying page after page of unmitigated gossip. For a period of time a few years ago I was a regular customer at a local supermarket. Each week as I approached the cashier I was confronted by a small magazine stand whose headlines promised to reveal sensational secrets from the lives of famous politicians, movie stars, and millionare tycoons. (Occasionally there would be instead an outlandish but harmless feature article on UFOs or wonder diet pills.) These periodicals cater to an appetite for gossip that only increases in people as it is fed. The fact that the eye is the medium of the sin rather than the ear makes it no less gossip and no less sinful. We should avoid such printed material as much as we avoid the juicy morsels about our neighbors spread by more local purveyors of gossip.

Busybodies

One of the worst type of gossips is a busybody. A busybody not only talks about inappropriate topics of conversation, but actively pries into others' affairs in order to offer unwanted advice, be the first branch on the local grapevine, and be recognized by all as "in the know." A busybody does not merely welcome provocative news as it presents itself and then proceed to transmit it to others; instead, like a prize reporter, the busybody follows tips and investigates promising stories, hoping to come up with a tantalizing headline. Also, like a self-certified general practitioner, the busybody has remedies for every problem and suggestions for every situation. The busybody tends to be an unpopular character, and rightly so.

There are two Greek words that are often translated as "busybody" in the New Testament. The first one is found in the following verse from 1 Peter 4:15:

But let none of you suffer as a murderer, or as a thief, or as an evil doer, or as *a busybody in other men's affairs.* (KJV)

Two modern versions of the Bible also use the word "busybody" in this passage (*The Living Bible, Phillips Modern English*), while other modern translations render the term with the expressions "mischief-maker" (RSV), "troublesome meddler" (NAS), and one who "tries to manage other people's business" (TEV). The Greek word (*allotri-episkopos*) literally means one who is overseeing or managing that which belongs to another. It refers to one who is trying to be an "*episkopos,*" a bishop or overseer, over that which does not rightfully belong under his charge. The central flaw in the behavior of an *allotri-episkopos* is his attempt to assume responsibility for that which has never been entrusted to him.

The second Greek word for busybody is found in two passages from the letters of Paul:

For we hear that some of you are living in idleness, mere *busybodies,* not doing any work. (2 Thes 3:11)

Besides that, they learn to be idlers, gadding about from house to house, and not only idlers but gossips and *busybodies,* saying what they should not. (1 Tm 5:13)

This word in Greek (*peri-ergazomai*) is derived from the verb that means "to work" (*ergazomai*).

In this context, the word refers to those who are energetic and industrious in supervising others' business and idle in managing their own. They are restless, consumed with curiosity and the desire to influence the lives of other people, preoccupied with matters that should not concern them, irresponsible in conducting their own affairs. Paul's exhortations to such people are "to do their own work in quietness and to earn their own living" (2 Thes 3:12), and to "aspire to live quietly, to mind your own affairs, and to work with your hands, as we charged you" (1 Thes 4:11). Paul urges the busybody to live in "quietness" (*hesuchia*), a word that means tranquility, peace, stillness, contentment. This is opposed to the foolish and restless babbling of gossip. He also summons the idler to "work with your hands"—saying, in other words, "Come, invest your efforts in constructive labor rather than wasting your boundless energy in interferring with the lives of others." Finally, he admonishes the busybody to "mind your own affairs"—as if to say, "Come, take responsibility for the things God has entrusted to you, and lay aside your compulsive preoccupation with the things that belong to others." Thus, we see that the two words used for "busybody" in the New Testament have roughly the same meaning: they both refer to a person who has a confused sense of rights and responsibilities, who minds others' affairs instead of his own.

A busybody will use every available opportunity

to probe into the lives and affairs of others. He will be curious about others' financial concerns, family squabbles, love life, problems, weaknesses, and sins. He will be eager to uncover hidden difficulties and quick to offer his solutions. And often, though not always, his own personal life will be in a shambles.

A busybody is also quick to offer opinions about situations he knows little of and bears no responsibility for. He will comment on the political and economic scene with the authority of an expert, though he has only read a weekly news summary and watched his favorite political interview show. He will freely criticize the pastor and elders of his church for the way they mishandle various ecclesiastical affairs, evaluating the work of committees which he has only heard of secondhand. He will lecture at length on how poorly various parents in the neighborhood raise their children, singling out families that he finds especially negligent. There is almost no area of life on which he will not eagerly and authoritatively render an opinion.

Of course, all of this is a caricature. There are a few pure-bred busybodies roaming restlessly about, but there are many ordinary people who occasionally dress like a busybody but then hastily change our clothes so as not to be recognized. We all have the potential to act as busybodies, and many of us regularly realize that potential. The key step, as in all such matters, is to recognize honestly one's wrongdoing and resolve by God's grace to change. The Lord does not want us to be busybodies or gossips any more than he wants us to be slanderers.

Friendship and Trust

Life works much better for all of us if we have people around with whom we can speak openly and personally. There are some elements of our lives that we can share only with a few trusted friends—and some of us find it difficult to share personally even in this context. However, our lives will probably be lonely and disturbed if we can trust no one with our sins, weaknesses, failures, ambitions, and deep desires.

Gossip destroys the bond of friendship. It makes it impossible for us to trust anyone with those matters which should not be blasted over the radio or read in the newspaper. Where gossip prevails, there relationships will be shallow and individuals isolated. Where gossip is uprooted and trust established, there shall be fulfilled the words of Psalm 133: "Behold, how good and pleasant it is when brothers dwell in unity!"

FOUR

Slapping with a Smile

HAVE YOU EVER had a friend joke casually about
your protruding wasteline or habitual tardi-
ness, and come away feeling slapped at and smiled
at in the same moment? Then you know what it is
like to be on the receiving end of what I call
"negative humor." Negative humor is often very
funny, but the laughs are purchased at someone's
expense. It is funny and painful at the same time.
Negative humor is like slapping someone with a
smile.

Negative humor often contains a slap at someone's mistakes, weaknesses, or eccentricities. The
following one-liners illustrate this type of humor:

Martha dances like a circus elephant.

Jeff eats so much that he needs to use his tool
chest as a lunch box.

Sally drives as though she thinks traffic signs
were merely ornaments to beautify the scenery.

Gary is so fat that he and his shadow make a
crowd.

Mary cooks so poorly that she can use her leftovers as household insecticide.

Carl's handwriting is so bad that you can't tell if he's trying to write a sentence or draw a picture.

Sometimes negative humor is used instead to poke fun at some embarrassing feature of another's personal life:

Well, Charlie, I see you are growing up quickly: popping pimples, cracking voice, five or six hairs on your chest—why, I supppose you'll have a girlfriend soon!

(As an adolescent I bore with many years of such jokes about the prominent fixture in the middle of my face that is an emblem of my semitic heritage.)

Sometimes negative humor is used affectionately as a way of kidding a friend with tongue-in-cheek by speaking of areas of strength as if they were areas of weakness:

Martha, you're the worst cook in this city. A man has to be courageous to eat your cooking. (Spoken to a woman whose actual excellence in the kitchen is unquestioned)

Carl is an unmitigated ignoramus. (Spoken of a man whose actual intellectual ability is known to all)

I am sure that I need not multiply examples of negative humor any further. It is a conversational pattern that is intimately familiar to all of us—both on the receiving and on the giving end.

Negative humor is not as serious a matter as slander or gossip. In fact, one is hard put to find any passages in the Bible that address the subject directly. However, the silence of scripture on the topic of negative humor can probably be explained by the differences between the culture of our day and that of biblical times. Negative humor thrives in social situations that are casual and informal, and modern Western society (especially American society) is far more casual and informal than the societies of Abraham, Moses, David, Ezra, and Jesus. Still, even if negative humor had been more common in the times of the prophets and apostles it would never have received the attention that scripture reserves for slander and gossip. Slander and gossip are serious offenses against God's law, for they involve the robbery of a person's most cherished possession—one's good name. Negative humor can be used in order to convey slander or gossip, but it is not always so used. Often negative humor is instead intended as a sign of affection or an indirect personal correction. But negative humor can cause significant problems in relationships and in individuals. If we want to reflect fully the love of God and impart life with our speech rather than death, we will seek to uproot negative humor from our relationships and learn how to smile without slapping.

The Purpose Behind the Slap

Negative humor can be used in many different ways to communicate many different messages. Sometimes the message is not really worth sending, and should be consigned to the garbage heap. However, sometimes the message *is* worth sending, and merely needs to be packaged in a more appropriate container.

Negative humor is often used to express affection, appreciation, and familiarity. We joke about another's weakness or eccentricity as a friend who knows them through and through. The fact that John snores like a train whistle and Phil can't hit a baseball out of the infield becomes a common store of jokes that anyone can pull out anytime and raise a laugh. The main intention behind such humor is to express unity, familiarity, friendship, affection, though often one can also find traces of competitiveness, jealousy, and one-upmanship.

A friend of mine recently told me of a custom in his job that demonstrates this manner of using negative humor. Whenever a member of the department retires, all of his immediate co-workers gather for a party held in his honor. A major feature of the evening's activity is a time to show appreciation by recounting the wildest mistakes the retiring worker has made in his many years of employment within the company. All chime in with funny stories showing how inept the fellow could be on occasion. The intention of the people in the department is to express appreciation, affection, and best-wishes, but the benevolent message is packaged in a purely negative container.

The prominent role played by negative humor in our society is in fact a commentary on some of the weaknesses of the society. We have lost a sense for how to show genuine affection, and consequently negative humor has become a primary vehicle for expressing friendship. Most of us are inhibited in showing physical affection outside of a sexual relationship, unlike people in many cultures who will walk down the street arm in arm, man with man, woman with woman, holding a warm conversation, building a relationship that is not sexually suspect. Most of us are also inhibited in showing verbal affection and are unable to give direct commendation or express in clear and sober language how much we esteem and value another person. Our society has largely lost the rich expressions of friendship and affection found in many other cultures, and has come to the point where negative humor is one of the main means of "building" a relationship.

However, negative humor does not really do the job. While conveying some affection, it at the same time sows seeds of criticalness and jealousy and resentment, and further acts as an obstacle to open and straightforward expression of affection. Therefore, we should avoid negative humor. But even more, we should cultivate positive forms of affection. We cannot transplant Mediterranean expressions of friendship unchanged into our inhibited Anglo-Saxon culture, but we can grow nonetheless in showing courtesy, honor, esteem, and affection with our bodies and our mouths. In this case, the message behind the negative humor should be largely retained, but it should be expressed in a new and more suitable form.

Negative humor is also used to administer correction. We joke about a friend or relative's mistake, failure, or weakness in order to coax them toward a change. For example, Mrs. Smith speaks to Mr. Smith while gazing through the kitchen window into the back of the house: "Our backyard is beginning to look like the city dump," meaning, "Would you please remember to take the trash out next week?" Then Mr. Smith, upon seeing Mrs. Smith pick up the telephone and begin dialing, speaks up: "I'm surprised that the telephone receiver hasn't yet fused to your ear," meaning, "Would you please use the telephone a little less often, especially when I am around?" The message is quite clear, but it's also very provocative.

Negative humor is a bad way to give correction for the same reason that it is a bad way to express affection. Negative humor is indirect rather than straightforward, negative and destructive rather than positive and constructive. If we want to correct someone, then we should go to them and tell them what we think should change. If we do not want to correct them, then we should keep our mouth sealed and refrain from expressing our annoyance or frustration through humor.

A third use of negative humor is to communicate

malice and contempt. Another word for this type of humor is "mockery." There is a Jewish tradition that only idols and sin should be mocked, based on Elijah's contest with the prophets of Baal at Mount Carmel. Elijah dared these prophets to call on their god to send fire from heaven to consume their sacrifices. They did so "from morning until noon" to no avail; Baal did not answer (1 Kgs 18:26). Then we read as follows:

> And at noon Elijah mocked them, saying, "Cry aloud, for he is a god; either he is musing, or he has gone aside [to relieve himself!], or he is on a journey, or perhaps he is asleep and must be awakened." (1 Kgs 18:27)

Elijah mocked Baal, intimating that he was not much of a god, if he were a god at all. The Jewish teaching was that such mockery is reserved for idols and sin (and perhaps for the prophets of false gods) and is inappropriate in any other situation or relationship. This teaching can also apply to us. In most ordinary cases mockery conveys a message which we just should not send, in this package or in any other.

Mockery is one of the greatest forms of dishonor and disrespect that can be shown. It is no coincidence that Jesus himself, the spotless lamb who bore the sins of the world, was mocked as well as scourged and crucified. The Roman soldiers played with him, crowning him with thorns, dressing him in a scarlet robe, handing him a reed for a scepter, and crying out, "Hail, King of the Jews!" The Romans mocked Jesus' kingship, and at the same time mocked the Jewish nation who would have such a powerful and dignified monarch. The Jewish soldiers played a different game:

> Now the men who were holding Jesus mocked him and beat him; they also blindfolded him and asked him, "Prophesy! Who is it that struck you?" And they spoke many other words against him, reviling him. (Lk 22:63-65)

As the Roman soldiers mocked Jesus' office as king, so the Jewish soldiers mocked his office as prophet. Jesus the Messiah and prophet of God, the eternal Son who shared in God's glory before the foundation of the world, completed the course of humiliation and self-emptying appointed for him by his Father, bearing the full shame and reproach and dishonor due the sin he bore on our behalf. He suffered to the utmost—not only physically, but also in the loss of his honor, which to a man of the first-century was worse than bodily torment. He lowered himself to the depths of suffering and humiliation that we might be ransomed from our sin and exalted with him in his resurrection and ascension to the very right hand of God. Jesus bore the mockery of men that we might be honored before the throne of God.

Unfortunately, many people use negative humor to show malice and contempt in situations that are clearly inappropriate. In his book *Strength Under Control,* John Keating recalls a boyhood acquaintance who suffered from a severe case of acne. His comrades made sure that his suffering was more than skin-deep by dubbing him with the nickname "pizza-face." This is simply another way of "reviling," a type of speech pattern strongly rebuked in the New Testament as excluding one from the Kingdom of God (1 Cor 5:11, 16:10). Contemptuous negative humor is only appropriate when one is mocking the Devil and his works; it is never appropriate as a form of personal attack.

In conclusion, we see that negative humor can be used to communicate affection, correction, or contempt, or perhaps some combination of the three. It is almost always an uncharitable and destructive form of communication, though at times it is not fully intended as such. There are better ways to show affection and give correction than through negative humor, and there are few occasions when contemptuous negative humor is appropriate. When we decide to put on Christian love, we should also decide to put off negative humor.

Consequences

The use of negative humor has many detrimental consequences. What appears at first sight to be harmless and playful jesting can, over time, produce emotional weakness and brittle, insecure relationships. Negative humor gives negative results.

The first consequence of negative humor is emotional insecurity. One can hear only so many jokes about one's appearance, intelligence, and abilities without starting to believe what others are saying. This is especially true for those who are emotionally sensitive and predisposed to a negative self-evaluation. Such insecurity can be expressed in timidity and self-denigration, in anger and aggression, or in a cold detached resentment.

A second consequence of negative humor is jealousy, criticalness, competitiveness. These arise through the natural desire to retaliate. "If Chuck feels free to cut me down like that, then he's going to get cut down himself." Sometimes such a response acts as a deterrent to further negative humor, but more often it ignites an escalating spiral of attack and counterattack. The tone throughout may be light and full of smiles, but the participants know they are actually in a battle. The relationships produced by such a sequence of interactions manifest little of the meekness, courtesy, and humble self-denying service that should characterize Christian personal relationships.

A third consequence of negative humor is inhibition in speaking openly, freely, and personally with others. We become reluctant to frankly discuss our weaknesses and failings or share about our problems, because this will give our comrades more sensitive material to use against us in their jibes. The cost of speaking freely about ourselves is far greater than the reward. An entrenched social pattern of negative humor also makes it difficult to frankly express our affection and sincere commendation. We are often tempted by our sense of awkwardness in such situations to add a negative wisecrack which removes with the left hand what we have just given with the right. Negative humor inhibits both the frank confession of personal need and the direct expression of honor and affection, two types of speech which help build truly Christian relationships.

A final consequence comes from negative humor's infectious and habit-forming nature: it can easily become the main way we relate to others. Negative humor can dominate us. A friend of mine once confessed to me, "When I first attempted to root out negative humor from my life, I often found myself strangely silent. Negative humor had become such a prominent feature of my relating to others that my attempts to put it aside made me feel like I was forsaking my native language and learning another." We learn how much negative humor dominates and pervades our speech only by trying to uproot it. Many of us will find that it is more pervasive than we think. Like flavorful potato chips, it is difficult to indulge in just a little bit of negative humor; you keep coming back for more. Unlike negative humor, potato chips are harmless in themselves; like negative humor, they can easily unbalance our diet and prevent us from ingesting more sound and healthy nourishment.

In quite a different context, Jesus said, "You will know them by their fruits" (Mt 7:16, 20). This also applies to negative humor. The fruit of negative humor is emotional insecurity, jealousy, rivalry, and the exclusion or inhibition of other more positive patterns of speech. Obviously, the tree that bears such fruit deserves the axe. If we are wise, that is precisely what we will give it.

Negative Humor and Positive Humor

A rejection of negative humor does not mean a rejection of all humor. Many forms of humor are joyful, healthy, and life-giving. I know several Christian men and women who are able to make a great contribution because of their sense of humor. Their jokes are constructive and positive as well as entertaining, and they exercise wisdom and restraint in using their gift at the proper times. Many fine Christian teachers exploit humor to press home important truths, and writers such as G.K. Chesterton and C.S. Lewis combine serious argument with amusing anecdotes. Humor can be enlisted in God's service if it is positive, joyful, and under control.

As I said earlier, negative humor is not as grave an offense as slander or gossip. In many situations we probably wouldn't even call it "sin." However, simple observation tells us that negative humor is habit-forming and a potential danger to our spiritual health. We are free to disregard the surgeon general's advice, but we will have to live with the consequences.

Bridled to Build

BOTH SCRIPTURE and experience teach us that our tongues can be deadly weapons. They can cause great damage in our own lives and in the lives of others. However, there is another side to our speech that must not be neglected: "Death and *life* are in the power of the tongue" (Prv 18:21). Just as the tongue can be used as a weapon producing death, so it can also be used as a means of imparting life. It can be an instrument of healing rather than a weapon for killing, a tool for construction rather than an implement for demolition. The tongue has great power, but that power can be used for good as well as evil.

There are three fundamental elements in the effective use of any instrument or tool. First, we must gain mastery over the tool so that it will serve us as we desire. The skilled artist has total control over his brush, the surgeon over his scalpel, the carpenter over his saw. Secondly, we must have a clear vision of the goal we are trying to attain, the work we want to do with the tool. Thirdly, we must know how to use the tool to reach the goal we are seeking. Our tool may be the best in the world, but without mastery, vision, and wisdom it will be of only limited value to us.

These three fundamental elements also apply to our use of the tongue. If our tongues are to be fruitful for God, then we must gain firm control over them, learn what he wants us to accomplish through them, and acquire practical knowledge on how the job is done. At that point our speech can begin to bear fruit worthy of God and his kingdom.

Bridling the Tongue

James chooses the image of the bridled horse to describe the mastery we need to exercise over our tongues:

> If anyone thinks he is religious, and does not bridle his tongue but deceives his heart, this man's religion is vain. (Jas 1:26)

He develops this image more fully in the third chapter:

> For we all make many mistakes, and if anyone makes no mistakes in what he says he is a perfect man, able to *bridle* the whole body *also*. If we put bits [literally, *bridles*] into the mouths of horses that they may obey us, we guide their whole bodies. (3:2-3)

The bridling of a horse is a fitting analogy for what needs to happen to our tongues. Our speech tends to be wild, impetuous, and resistent to control, like a strong and stubborn stallion. If the strength of the stallion is to be put to any constructive use, the horse must first be broken and bridled. It must learn to follow the directions of its master rather than its own willful impulses. Similarly, our tongues must be broken and bridled if they are to serve us as useful tools for imparting life to others and building up the body of Christ.

The bridling of the tongue has both a negative and a positive side. On the negative side, we need to restrain ourselves from speaking too hastily and too extensively. On the positive side, we need to direct our speech so that it gives strength to others. Our ultimate goal is not merely to check and restrain the tongue but to harness its power for the service of the kingdom.

The Negative Side. We begin with the need for restraint. Scripture is full of exhortations to be thoughtful, careful, and moderate in our speech, and to avoid rash and hasty words. We are also cautioned to avoid long-winded speech. The following passages illustrate the biblical teaching:

> The mind of the righteous ponders how to answer,
>> but the mouth of the wicked pours out evil things. (Prv 12:28)

If one gives answer before he hears,
   it is his folly and shame. (Prv 18:13)

Do you see a man who is hasty in his words?
   There is more hope for a fool than for him.
                                      (Prv 29:20)

A fool multiplies words. (Eccl 10:14a)

Let every man be quick to hear, slow to speak,
   slow to anger. (Jas 1:19)

As usual, Sirach contributes an insight that is both
amusing and thought-provoking: "The mind of
fools is in their mouth, but the mouth of wise men
is in their mind" (Sir 21:26). In other words, the
fool speaks without giving proper thought to what
he is saying; his mind is subordinate to his tongue.
The wise man, on the other hand, speaks carefully
and prudently, judging when his words will benefit his hearers in some way; his tongue is subordinate to his mind. This is the consensus of
scripture: a hasty word is a foolish word.

We see in the gospels that the apostle Peter had
a problem with rash speech. At first his quickness
of response appears to his credit. When Jesus asks
his disciples, "Who do you say that I am?" it is
Peter who gives the inspired reply, "You are the
Christ, the Son of the living God" (Mt 16:13-16).
From this point on, however, his rash remarks get
him into trouble. Immediately following Peter's
confession, Jesus begins to tell his disciples about

his approaching death in Jerusalem. With fresh confidence drawn from the Lord's commission to him as the rock (Mt 16:17-19), Peter audaciously rebukes his Master and contradicts his words:

> And Peter took him and began to rebuke him, saying, "God forbid, Lord! This shall never happen to you." But he turned and said to Peter, "Get behind me, Satan! You are a hindrance to me; for you are not on the side of God, but of men." (Mt 16:22-23)

Peter's rash words are again shown to be foolish in an incident that probably followed soon after his rebuke. Jesus takes Peter, James, and John up a mountain where he is gloriously transfigured before the disciples and converses with Moses and Elijah. Obviously enthralled and eager to meet Moses and Elijah himself, Peter rashly approaches Jesus with a request:

> And as the men were parting from him, Peter said to Jesus, "Master, it is well that we are here; let us make three booths, one for you and one for Moses and one for Elijah"—*not knowing what he said.* As he said this, a cloud came and overshadowed them; and they were afraid as they entered the cloud. And a voice came out of the cloud, saying, "This is my Son, my Chosen; listen to him!" And when the voice had spoken, Jesus was found alone. (Lk 9:33-36a)

Peter was preoccupied with Moses and Elijah; but the voice from heaven said, "This is my *Son*, listen to *him!*" Peter's rash words had again gone astray.

On the night of Jesus' betrayal and arrest, Peter again speaks impulsive words, again contradicting his Master. Jesus and his disciples had finished their meal and had walked together to the Mount of Olives.

> Then Jesus said to them, "You will all fall away because of me this night; for it is written, 'I will strike the shepherd, and the sheep will be scattered.' But after I am raised up, I will go before you to Galilee." Peter declared to him, "Though they all fall away because of you, I will never fall away." Jesus said to him, "Truly, I say to you, this very night, before the cock crows, you will deny me three times." Peter said to him, "Even if I must die with you, I will not deny you." And so said all the disciples.
>
> (Mt 26:31-35)

Peter, the one who boasts so loudly and impetuously of his unquenchable loyalty to his Master to the point of contradicting his Master's prophetic words, is singled out for a special humiliation. The other disciples "fall away," but only Peter explicitly denies the Lord, and that he does three times. The denial itself again manifests Peter's problem with rash words, though this time he responds from the impulse of fear rather than enthusiasm (Mt 26:69-75). Peter's humble and sincere repentance (Mt 26:75), combined with his encounter with the risen Lord and his experience of the purifying power of the Holy Spirit, appear to cure him of his habitual problem with rash words. After the resurrection of Christ and the day of Pentecost, Peter looks like a new man.

Many of our problems with hasty speech spring from an underlying emotional difficulty such as anxiety or insecurity. Many people have an emotional compulsion to talk—quickly, hastily, and at great length—and feel incapable of controlling the desire. Sometimes such a speech pattern is part of a broader cluster of control problems (sex, food, drink, etc.) that all have a common emotional root. Often the discouraged conviction that we cannot change these patterns is itself a manifestation of the underlying emotional problem. The conviction is false and deceptive. However, the way to effect change is not merely through more concentrated willpower; the emotional difficulty must be squarely confronted if lasting change is to occur.

We also need to experience the grace and power of God if we are to change patterns of rash speech. This fact is implicit in the opening prayer of Psalm 141:

Set a guard over my mouth, O Lord,
    keep watch over the door of my lips!
                              (Ps 141:3)

The same image is taken up in Sirach 22:27:

> O that a guard were set over my mouth,
>   and a seal of prudence upon my lips,
> that it may keep me from falling,
>   so that my tongue may not destroy me!

As a soldier guards the gates of a city or a palace to prevent the wrong people from entering or exiting, so we ask the Lord to guard the door of our mouth to keep us from uttering unrighteous words. We certainly need to stand guard ourselves (Prv 13:3), but our efforts alone will be inadequate. We need the help of the power of God.

The Positive Side. The bridling of the tongue has a positive side as well as a negative side. We need to develop right patterns of speech as well as to restrain wrong ones. A horse is bridled in order to harness and channel his power, not merely to keep him from running wildly away. Similarly, we should gain mastery over our tongues so that they might be used as instruments with which we can glorify God.

As stated earlier, our words can be a source of life as well as a source of death. The following proverbs illustrate the view held by scripture:

> The mouth of the righteous is a fountain of life.
>   (Prv 10:11a)

> The tongue of the wise brings healing.
>   (Prv 12:18b)

A gentle tongue is a tree of life. (Prv 15:4)

There are several other passages which show the goodness of speaking the right word at the right time:

> To make an apt answer is a joy to a man,
>   and a word in season, how good it is!
>   (Prv 15:23)

> A word fitly spoken
>   is like apples of gold in a setting of silver.
>   (Prv 25:11)

> For everything there is a season, and a time for every matter under heaven . . . a time to keep silence, and a time to speak. (Eccl 3:1, 7b)

Sirach not only praises the right word given at the right time, but urges us to speak when we have this word: "Do not refrain from speaking at the crucial time, and do not hide your wisdom" (4:23). There are times when we have an obligation to speak; thus, our silence on some occasions can be as culpable as our unruly speech is on others. This is an important point to grasp, for we often think of self-control merely in negative terms—it restrains us from doing what we are not supposed to do. We often neglect the more positive dimension of the bridle. Some of us have imbibed a distorted image of the model Christian, one that portrays him as a quiet, inexpressive, retiring monk or Puritan (though few of the monks I have met actually fit this picture, and I imagine that such would also be the case with the venerable old Puritans). This is a false picture of ideal Christian character. Though we should be capable of silence and docility, we should also be capable of aggressive action. If we have truly bridled our tongue, then we will be able to speak at the proper time and thereby contribute constructively to the various situations in which we find ourselves.

Just as an emotional difficulty sometimes underlies a problem with rash speech, so emotional factors often underlie a problem with a reluctance to speak. The real problem is often not unwillingness but an emotional difficulty with shyness, timidity, and fear. With faith and resolution these problems can be overcome. It is necessary to recognize when the problem arises from sheer unwillingness and when it has an emotional root. The cure for unwillingness is repentance; the cure for an emotional problem involves a more significant internal change.

The first step in effectively utilizing a tool is to gain control over its use. Therefore, the first step in the process of learning to give life with our tongues is to gain mastery over them. Like a soldier with his troops or an overseer with his laborers, we need to assume a position of authority over our speech so that we might succeed in our war against sin and in our building up of the body of Christ. Our tongues must be broken and bridled so as to prove productive and fruitful in the service of Christ.

Speech That Builds Up

Self-control is not an end in itself. It is valuable insofar as it allows us to be the kind of people the Lord wants us to be. A man or woman may be perfectly self-controlled and morally corrupt at the same time. In fact, self-control can allow one to do greater works of unrighteousness than one would otherwise be capable of, just as it also can allow one to serve the Lord with greater success. Adolph Hitler and Joseph Stalin may have been paragons of self-mastery, but this quality would have only equipped them to be more productive in the works of evil.

This truth applies fully to the area of speech. It is possible to have perfect mastery over one's speech and then use it for an evil end. Furthermore, it is possible to be master of one's speech, have a noble goal, and at the same time lack the wisdom to know how to attain that goal. Bridling the tongue is only the first step; now that you are ready to ride, you must decide on your destination and how to get there.

What is the goal for the use of our speech? The apostle Paul states it succinctly:

> Let no evil talk come out of your mouths, but only such as is good for *edifying,* as fits the occasion, that it may impart grace to those who hear. (Eph 4:29)

> Let all things be done for *edification.* (1 Cor 14:26b)

The goal of our speech is *edification*. This old English word is connected to the word "edifice," which simply means a building; the verb is often translated elsewhere as "build," "build up," or "upbuild." The Greek word literally means to construct a building. It is used in this literal sense in many passages of scripture (see, for example, Mt 23:29; Lk 12:18; Jn 2:20). Paul uses it in its figurative sense to indicate the goal of our speech, and of all we do.

Underlying this image of "edification" or "building up" is the New Testament view of the church as the temple or building of God (Mt 16:18; 1 Cor 3:9-17; 2 Cor 6:16; Eph 2:19-22; 1 Pt 2:4-8). The body of the individual Christian is also seen as a temple or building (1 Cor 6:15-20). Paul probably chose this image for two reasons. First, it conveys the truth that God lives in Christians, both individually and corporately, just as his presence dwelt in the temple in Jerusalem under the old dispensation. We have all the privileges of those who minister in the inner tent—freedom of access and continual worship. We also bear the responsibilities incumbent on those who minister in the inner tent—the call to perfect holiness (2 Cor 7:1). Secondly, the image of the temple or building allows Paul to impress upon us our current state of being "under construction." The foundation has been laid and the cornerstone set, but the building is not yet complete (1 Cor 3:9-11; Eph 2:19-22; 1 Pt 2:4-5). More work needs to be done on us, individually and corporately, before we become the temple he fully desires.

This second aspect of the temple image provides the background to Paul's use of the term "build up." Each of us is called to participate in the building up of the body of Christ: "Strive to excel in *building up* the church" (1 Cor 14:12). We build up the church by strengthening its individual members, fostering its common life, and adding to its numbers. When we do these things we are actually sharing in a work that is central to God's purpose in human history, as revealed by Paul in his letter to the Ephesians:

> And his gifts were that some should be apostles, some prophets, some evangelists, some pastors and teachers, to equip the saints for the work of ministry, for *building up the body of Christ,* until we all attain to the unity of the faith and of the knowledge of the Son of God, to mature manhood, to the measure of the stature of the fullness of Christ. (4:11-13; see also 1:9-10, 22-23, 2:11-22, and 3:8-10)

God is intent on erecting this building, and he has made us part of the edifice and enlisted us in its continuing construction.

Now we can grasp the meaning of Paul's teaching in Ephesians 4:29: "Let no evil talk come out of your mouths, but only such as is good for *edifying.*" God has called each of us to share in his work of building up a people. One of the more powerful tools at our disposal is our tongue. Paul therefore urges us to wield this tool deftly in God's service. Our speech should be used to strengthen our fellow Christians, enrich the common life of the people of God, and bring others to a knowledge of Christ and a place in his body.

The force that controls our work of building up the body (and therefore controls our speech) is Christian love. Paul regularly connects love and edification:

> "Knowledge" puffs up, but *love builds up*.
> (1 Cor 8:1)

> Rather, *speaking the truth in love,* we are to grow up in every way into him who is the head, into Christ, from whom the whole body, joined and knit together by every joint with which it is supplied, when each part is working properly, makes bodily growth and *upbuilds itself in love*.
> (Eph 4:15-16)

In other words, the way that we build up the body of Christ is by living and walking and speaking in love. It is by looking out for one another's good rather than our own, even as Jesus himself looked out for our good at the cost of his life:

> Let each of us please his neighbor *for his good, to edify him*. For Christ did not please himself; but, as it is written, "The reproaches of those who reproached thee fell on me." (Rom 15:2-3)

First Corinthians 14, which teaches us how to use our tongue in the Christian assembly, employs the word "edify" more than any other chapter of scripture, and the fact that it follows directly on Paul's great praise of Christian love in 1 Corinthians 13 reveals important connections in Paul's mind: Our speech is governed by our call to build up the body of Christ, and our work of building is controlled by Christian love. When we speak the truth in love, we build up the body of Christ.

The God-appointed destination of our speech, then, is the building up of the body of Christ in love. But how do we get there? How do we live this out? We need practical wisdom about how to speak in love. We need a road map to guide us. Yet, while this practical wisdom is certainly important, it is less important than actually bridling our tongue and commiting ourselves to use it for the building up of the body of Christ in love. This is the indispensable beginning of our work.

SIX

A Tongue Seasoned
with Grace

A VERSE from the writings of the apostle Paul can serve as a good beginning for our attempt to apply his other exhortations about upbuilding speech:

> Let your speech always be gracious, seasoned with salt, so that you may know how you ought to answer every one. (Col 4:6)

The emphasis in this verse falls on the word "gracious." Our speech should "always be gracious." A related direction is also found in Paul's main summons to speak in a way that builds up:

> Let no evil talk come out of your mouths, but only such as is good for *edifying,* as fits the occasion, that it may impart *grace* to those who hear. (Eph 4:29)

Gracious speech is speech that imparts grace— God's grace, of course, but also our own. One of the keys to having your speech always build up is to have "your speech always be gracious."

Gracious words show favor, affection, concern. They are positive, constructive, and full of substance. They are "seasoned with salt" rather than tasteless and insipid. Even a hard word can be digested well when it is flavored with the right portion of grace.

Gracious speech strengthens personal relationships. Friendship, commitment, and trust flourish where gracious words are found. This is part of the message conveyed in the following proverb:

> He who loves purity of heart,
> and whose speech is gracious, will have the
> king as his friend. (Prv 22:11)

The king will choose as his trusted counsellors and friends those whose speech is courteous, joyful, and wise. Gracious words inspire confidence and trust.

We can learn to speak graciously by embracing the characteristics of gracious speech. Let us now look at five of them.

1. Expressing Praise and Affection

While discussing negative humor in an earlier chapter I pointed out how many of us find it difficult to show direct affection. Most of us are inhibited in expressing praise and love to others. We find it hard to commend others for their virtue, diligence, or ability. Nonetheless, the expression of commendation and affection is an integral element of gracious speech.

The apostle Paul consistently shows grace and favor in just this way. He is generous, even lavish, in giving praise and expressing affection. Consider the following words of commendation delivered to whole churches:

I thank my God through Jesus Christ for all of you, because your faith is proclaimed in all the world. (Rom 1:8)

I myself am satisfied about you, my brethren, that you yourselves are full of goodness, filled with all knowledge, and able to instruct one another. (Rom 15:14)

I give thanks to God always for you because of the grace of God which was given you in Christ Jesus, that in every way you were enriched in him with all speech and all knowledge—even as the testimony to Christ was confirmed among you—so that you are not lacking in any spiritual gift. (1 Cor 1:4-7a)

But concerning love of the brethren you have no need to have any one write to you, for you yourselves have been taught by God to love one another; and indeed you do love all the brethren throughout Macedonia. (1 Thes 4:9-10a)

Paul also honors individuals by praising their merits to others. In the following passage from

Philippians 2, Paul praises Timothy and Epaphroditus, two of his fellow workers and helpers, to the Christians at Philippi:

> I hope in the Lord Jesus to send Timothy to you soon, so that I may be cheered by news of you. I have no one like him, who will be genuinely anxious for your welfare. . . . Timothy's worth you know, how as a son with a father he has served with me in the gospel. . . .
>
> I have thought it necessary to send to you Epaphroditus my brother and fellow worker and fellow soldier. . . . So receive him in the Lord with all joy; and honor such men, for he nearly died for the work of Christ, risking his life to complete your service to me.
>
> (Phil 2:19-20, 22, 25, 29-30)

Paul is also uninhibited in expressing his affection with words:

> It is right for me to feel thus about you all, because I hold you in my heart, for you are all partakers with me of grace, both in my imprisonment and in the defense and confirmation of the gospel. For God is my witness, how I yearn for you all with the affection of Christ Jesus.
>
> (Phil 1:7-8)

Therefore, my brethren, whom I love and long for, my joy and crown, stand firm thus in the Lord, my beloved. (Phil 4:1)

You are in our hearts, to die together and to live together. I have great confidence in you; I have great pride in you; I am filled with comfort. With all our affliction, I am overjoyed.

(2 Cor 7:3b-4)

The apostle whose writings constitute a sizable portion of the New Testament thus provides an excellent model of gracious speech.

When I first became a Christian I believed that it was wrong to praise people for their qualities and gifts. Since we are weak and sinful and God is the source of all good things, I reasoned, it insults God's beneficence to praise a human being. Praise also might provide an unnecessary pretext for ego-inflation, pride, and vanity, or so I thought. I therefore avoided praising others, and when others praised me I recoiled like a child who touches a hot stove. However, my friends quickly persuaded me that these ideas lacked a solid biblical foundation. In fact, the biblical evidence was all stacked on the other side. According to scripture, we are to build one another up with gracious speech, including commendation and the expression of affection.

To praise people directly and before others is to give them a valuable gift. This strengthens them and imparts confidence and courage, as well as increasing the esteem in which others hold them. As "a good name is better than precious ointment" (Eccl 7:1a), so our giving of honor with our tongues can be more precious than a material gift. We should desire to be generous in the giving of such gifts, so that we might enrich one another and strengthen one another in the service of the Kingdom of God.

As with all things, it is possible to give praise or show affection in ways that are wrong or unhelpful. Affection can degenerate into maudlin sentimentality, leading us to think excessively about how we feel about others and how others feel about us. Commendation can degenerate into empty flattery or a compulsive desire to please. The need for balance in the area of praise is conveyed by the biblical analogy of honey. In Proverbs 16:24, gracious speech is compared to honey, since they both bring pleasure and health:

> Pleasant words are like a honey comb,
>   sweetness to the soul and health to the body.

In Proverbs 25:27, gracious speech is again compared to honey, but this time the proverb recommends moderation in its use:

> It is not good to eat much honey,
>   so be sparing of complimentary words.

We can often spoil the effect of our praise by overstatement, excessively verbose compliments, or too frequent commendation. This should not discourage us from giving praise and showing affection—the honey is still sweet to the taste and strengthening and energizing to the body. However, we must learn wisdom in order to couch our gracious words in proper form and in proper measure.

2. Correcting with Meekness

The example of the apostle Paul can also show us that our speech should not always be commendatory. There is a time and place for correction and severity. Yet even our correction and instruction should be done graciously.

Before turning to Paul's example, let us look at his teaching. He has this to say about giving correction:

> Brethren, if a man is overtaken in any trespass, you who are spiritual should restore him in a spirit of gentleness [meekness]. (Gal 6:1)

> And the Lord's servant must not be quarrelsome but kindly to every one, an apt teacher, forbearing, correcting his opponents with gentleness [meekness]. (2 Tm 2:24-25a)

The Greek word for "gentleness" or "meekness" used in these passages could also be translated "courtesy." Paul is concerned that correction not be administered in an arrogant, heavy-handed manner, but with humility and self-control, always looking out first for the good of the other person. Severity may be required, and we should be free enough from concern about others' opinions to be severe at the proper time; but all must be done in the service of Christ and our brethren, and not in slavery to our own fleshly anger and self-will.

We have a good example of Paul's gracious correction in his first letter to the Corinthians. The Corinthian church was in great need of correction. It was tolerating divisions and dissensions (1:10-13), jealousy and strife (3:1-4), sexual immorality (5:1-5), intra-church legal action before pagan judges (6:1-8), idolatrous feasts (10:14-22), and disorder in the common assembly (11:17-22). Paul vigorously corrects these abuses and exhorts the Corinthians to repent and change. His tone is firm but not strident, admonishing but not unrelievedly critical. He begins the letter by complimenting the Corinthian Christians on their abundance of spiritual gifts. In his rebukes he speaks as a concerned father to his undisciplined children:

I do not write this to make you ashamed, but to admonish you as my beloved children. For though you have countless guides in Christ, you do not have many fathers. For I became your father in Christ Jesus through the gospel. I urge you, then, be imitators of me. (1 Cor 4:14-16)

He eagerly gives commendation where commendation is due: "I commend you because you remember me in everything and maintain the traditions even as I delivered them to you" (1 Cor 11:2). But then he proceeds to offer correction freely and without inhibition: "But in the following instructions I do not commend you, because when you come together it is not for the better but for the worse" (1 Cor 11:17). In this letter Paul follows admirably his own advice to restore a fallen brother or sister "in a spirit of gentleness" (Gal 6:1).

Paul corrects the Galatian church with greater severity. Their problems are more serious than moral lapses, as in Corinth; the Galatians are in danger of misunderstanding and distorting the essence of the gospel message itself (1:6-9, 5:2-4). Unlike his other letters, this one contains no introductory thanksgiving prayer. Paul moves immediately into a discussion of his concerns about the Galatians, presenting them directly and with force: "O foolish Galatians! Who has bewitched you, before whose eyes Jesus Christ was publicly portrayed as crucified?" (Gal 3:1). Yet even this letter, written in such heat, pulses with a deep personal concern and commitment (Gal 4:12-20). Paul does not speak from mere defensiveness, irritation, and annoyance, but instead admonishes the Galatians with a father's concern to see his children walking in righteousness and truth. Even here Paul's correction is gracious and seasoned with salt.

Just as we can build one another up with expressions of praise and affection, so we can build one another up with correction administered at the proper time and in the proper manner. This delicacy may not be appreciated with its first swallow, but it will eventually be recognized for what it is: one of the most nutritious and well-seasoned meals available.

3. Communicating Faith and Joy

The best way to communicate faith and joy to others is through our speech. Our speech not only reflects how we are approaching our lives, but also contributes to how others will approach theirs. If our speech is positive and filled with faith in God and joy in the Holy Spirit, then others will experience this and be strengthened in the same qualities. If our speech is negative and filled with anxiety, discouragement, and complaint, we will contribute to the erosion of our listeners' faith and joy. The communication of a positive Christian attitude to life is an essential component of gracious speech.

The damaging power of discouraged, negative speech is well illustrated in the mission of the twelve spies found in the book of Numbers. While still encamped in the wilderness Moses sent twelve men to spy out and report on the strengths and weaknesses and prominent features of the land of Canaan and its peoples. All of the spies except Joshua and Caleb returned thoroughly intimidated by the power of the Canaanites. Forgetting the call and promise of the Lord, they spoke disheartening words to the people:

But Caleb quieted the people before Moses, and said, "Let us go up at once, and occupy it; for we are well able to overcome it." Then the men who had gone up with him said, "We are not able to go up against the people; for they are stronger than we." So they brought to the people of Israel an evil report of the land which they had spied out, saying, "The land, through which we have gone, to spy it out, is a land that devours its inhabitants; and all the people that we saw in it are men of great stature. And there we saw the Nephilim . . . and we seemed to ourselves like grasshoppers, and so we seemed to them."

Then all the congregation raised a loud cry; and the people wept that night. And all the people of Israel murmured against Moses and Aaron; the whole congregation said to them, "Would that we had died in the land of Egypt! Or would that we had died in this wilderness! Why does the Lord bring us into this land, to fall by the sword? Our wives and our little ones will become a prey; would it not be better for us to go back to Egypt?"

And they said to one another, "Let us choose a captain, and go back to Egypt."

(Nm 13:30-14:4)

The Lord had accomplished signs and wonders on behalf of his people, delivering them from bondage in Egypt, judging their oppressors, feeding them in the wilderness, and speaking to them amid fire and cloud from Mount Sinai. Now the time had come for the fulfillment of the promise made to Abraham four centuries past, the promise that his descendants would inherit the land of his sojournings. But instead of calling the people forward to possess by faith the land promised to their forefathers, the spies yield to their anxiety and discouragement and speak words that dishearten the people and cause them to murmur against their deliverer and to plot together to return to the land of bondage. The Lord responds with understandable anger, and the people are only spared through the intercession of Moses; even so, they must bear their punishment and wander in the wilderness for forty years until a new generation arises that will be more worthy to receive the promised inheritance.

How often do we respond to problems or obstacles in our lives with discouragement and unbelief, like the ten cowardly and faithless spies? And how often does our discouragement get communicated to others, so that others refuse to seize the land of promise as we do? For most of us the answer is, "All too often." Instead of responding with discouragement, we should take as our models Caleb and Joshua:

And Joshua the son of Nun and Caleb the son of Jephunneh, who were asong those who had spied out the land, rent their clothes, and said to all the congregation of the people of Israel,

"The land, which we passed through to spy it out, is an exceedingly good land. If the Lord delights in us, he will bring us into this land and give it to us, a land which flows with milk and honey. Only, do not rebel against the Lord; and do not fear the people of the land, for they are bread for us; their protection is removed from them, and the Lord is with us; do not fear them." (Nm 14:6-9)

Caleb and Joshua responded to the challenge with courage and faith, and sought to impart that same courage and faith to others through their words. The challenges we face differ from theirs, but our response should be the same—courage and faith. Our words should communicate these attitudes to others.

It is easy to fall into a pattern of grumbling and complaining—complaints about the boss, and complaints about the kids; complaints about food, and complaints about drink; complaints about weather, and complaints about health; complaints about time pressure, and complaints about fatigue. Negative speech about our circumstances seems to come naturally to our fallen flesh. Nonetheless, the Lord wants us to break free from the old nature and put on the new nature, "which is being renewed in knowledge after the image of its creator" (Col 3:10). Grumbling, discouraged words do not impart grace to those who hear, and therefore they have no place in the speech program of the Kingdom of God. This program is based on faith in Jesus Christ and his resurrection, and on hope in the inheritance that will be ours when he returns:

> Blessed be the God and Father of our Lord Jesus Christ! By his great mercy we have been born anew to a living hope through the resurrection of Jesus Christ from the dead, and to an inheritance which is imperishable, undefiled, and unfading, kept in heaven for you, who by God's power are guarded through faith for a salvation ready to be revealed in the last time. In this you rejoice, though now for a little while you may have to suffer various trials, so that the genuineness of your faith, more precious than gold which though perishable is tested by fire, may redound to praise and glory and honor at the revelation of Jesus Christ. Without having seen him you love him; though you do not now see him you rejoice with unutterable and exalted joy. As the outcome of your faith you obtain the salvation of your souls. (1 Pt 1:3-9)

Our speech should reflect our confidence in God's saving and protecting power, and should impart to others a similar confidence. Words of faith can dispel anxiety; words of hope can overcome despair.

I am not advocating here a Polyanna or head-in-the-sand approach to problems. We all need to learn how to recognize problems and talk about them in the right way. There are times when we are emotionally overwhelmed and need some way of expressing our difficulty in words. In such cases, I have used the following format in sharing with close friends my frustrations and difficulties: "Look, John, I know that the thoughts going through my head are nonsense. I don't really believe them. I know that the Lord is with me and will give me his help. But this is how I'm feeling now." I then proceed to tell my friend what I am experiencing. I expect at the end to receive words of encouragement and perhaps correction from him. I have expressed my problem, but I have also acknowledged the realities of the situation and the truths by which I am committed to live.

There is a time for directly and honestly talking about our problems and difficulties. However, such talk should not dominate our conversation. Instead, our speech should be filled with words of faith, confidence, and joy. Such words impart grace to others, and allow us to appropriate more grace ourselves.

4. Making Peace

Another facet of gracious speech has to do with conflict situations. According to Sirach, "a fool is ungracious and abusive" (18:18). To be ungracious is to be contentious, argumentative, impatient, defensive, and critical. By contrast, the gracious man or woman is patient, slow to anger, undefensive, and eager to follow the apostle Paul's exhortation, "So far as it depends on you, live peaceably with all" (Rom 12:18).

There are many passages in scripture that urge us to be gracious and meek in our speech rather than willful and contentious. Proverbs 15:1 focuses especially on how we should respond to one who is angry with us:

> A soft answer turns away wrath
> but a harsh word stirs up anger.

We should not ordinarily return anger for anger, since blow will follow blow and the skirmish will escalate into a war. Paul's letters to Timothy and Titus are filled with similar instructions, applying particularly to controversy and dissension:

> Remind them of this, and charge them before the Lord to avoid *disputing with words,* which does no good, but only ruins the hearers.
> (2 Tm 2:14)

> Have nothing to do with stupid, senseless controversies; you know that they breed *quarrels.* And the Lord's servant must not be *quarrelsome* but kindly to every one, an apt teacher, forbearing, correcting his opponents with gentleness. (2 Tm 2:23-25a)

> Remind them to be submissive to rulers and authorities, to be obedient, to be ready for any honest work, to speak evil of no one, to avoid *quarreling,* to be gentle, and to show perfect courtesy toward all men. (Ti 3:1-2)

The Greek words translated here as "disputing" and "quarreling" all derive from the same word—a military term referring to a fight, battle, or combat. Paul thus urges against using our speech to contend with one another. Instead, we are exhorted to be kindly, meek, forbearing, ready to show perfect courtesy to all. In short, Paul teaches us to be gracious.

There is a place and a time for a firm statement of one's convictions and an argument on their behalf. Paul contended with Peter in Antioch (Gal 2:11-14), and fought zealously for his understanding of the gospel at the Council of Jerusalem (Gal 2:1-5). He also argued with other Jews in the synagogue about the interpretation of scripture and the identity of the Messiah (Acts 17:1-4). Jesus himself disputed with the religious leaders of his day, and denounced them forcefully (Mt 23:1-39). However, this is not supposed to be the main way that we relate to others, especially to those with whom we share a committed relationship. Our relationships and our speech patterns should mainly be characterized by meekness, patience, and grace. (See *Strength Under Control* by John Keating, a book in the *Living as a Christian* series, for more discussion of meekness and aggressiveness in scripture and the Christian life.)

For a Jewish man like myself, this has been a hard lesson to learn. The people of Israel are often described in scripture as "stubborn and stiff-necked." Many of my people (including myself) have maintained these traits even to the present. The old joke captures something of the truth: "Where there are two Jews, there are three opinions." I grew up with a taste for debate and heated discussion, and I would often defend positions in which I did not really believe merely "for the sake of argument." I *enjoyed* verbal conflict. I held to my opinions, however absurd, with an intransigent will. As you can imagine, I was not always a pleasant guy to have around. When I first came to a personal knowledge of God and faith in Jesus the Messiah, the Lord began to work on this area immediately. I began to see clearly how this habitual speech pattern damaged my closest relationships and produced tension rather than peace. I believe I have grown considerably "in grace" and self-control over the years, though my Jewish forthrightness and love for discussion and debate have not been totally lost.

A Christian man or woman should be strong, confident, and able to face conflict without being fearful or intimidated. A Christian man or woman should also be ready and able to stand up for righteousness and truth at the proper time, even when such action is costly. However, a Christian should not primarily approach relationships in terms of struggle and conflict, but should instead seek to "live peaceably with all." Such a one has learned the meaning of gracious words and has seasoned his speech with salt.

5. Showing Courtesy

Another important element of gracious speech is courtesy: "A pleasant voice multiplies friends, and a gracious tongue multiplies courtesies" (Sir 6:5). As we have already seen, Paul instructs Christians to "show perfect courtesy toward all men" (Ti 3:2). If our tongues are to be consistently upbuilding to others, we must learn to speak with courtesy.

The English word "courteous" has two different meanings which should be distinguished from one another. The older meaning, as formulated in Webster's, is as follows: "marked by polished manners, gallantry, or ceremonial usage of a court." This use of "courtesy" draws negative reactions from many modern people. We think of the formalities and ceremonies that only an idle aristocracy of a bygone day could have observed patiently. This reaction can color our attitude toward all "manners" and "etiquette." However, the second dictionary definition of "courteous" has a different focus: "marked by respect for and consideration of others." When "manners" and "etiquette" are working properly they function not merely as empty forms, but as customs that express mutual respect and consideration among a grouping of people.

I know of three simple yet significant ways that we should express courtesy in our conversation. First of all, we should listen attentively when others are speaking. To let your eyes or thoughts wander aimlessly or to fall asleep while someone is speaking is to be discourteous.

Secondly, we should not interrupt another while he is speaking. This action is condemned in both Proverbs and Sirach:

> If one gives answer before he hears,
>   it is his folly and shame. (Prv 18:13)

> Do not answer before you have heard,
>   nor interrupt a speaker in the midst of his
>   words. (Sir 11:8)

In the Qumran community of Jesus' day one endured a penalty of ten days penitential discipline for interrupting a companion while he was speaking.

Thirdly, we should take interest in the lives of others rather than simply talking about ourselves. We should be eager to learn more about others, and we should show genuine interest and concern in what interests and concerns them. All three of these practices entail a subordination of our own thoughts, desires, and interests to those of another. They oppose self-concern and express our character as humble servants: "Let each of you look not only to his own interests, but also to the interests of others" (Phil 2:4).

Courtesy is an essential part of gracious speech. If our words are to build others up and give them grace, they must be spoken with respect and consideration for others. Like Jesus himself, we should seek to please our neighbor "for his good, to edify him"(Rom 15:2-3).

Building One Another Up

The five aspects of gracious speech discussed in this chapter are all integral to our building one another up in love. They are some of the most crucial practical and positive expressions of loving speech available to us. If the goal of our speech is to build one another up in love, and the precondition for its attainment is a bridled tongue, then these elements of gracious speech are the road we should set out on in order to reach our destination.

A Tongue That Glorifies God

THE LORD JESUS CHRIST summarized the intent of the law and the prophets in the following words:

> You shall love the Lord your God with all your heart, and with all your soul, and with all your mind. This is the great and first commandment. And a second is like it, You shall love your neighbor as yourself. On these two commandments depend all the law and the prophets.
>
> (Mt 22:37-40)

To this point we have focused on how to use our speech to fulfill the second great commandment: we love our neighbor with our tongue when we speak in a gracious and upbuilding manner. In this final chapter we will turn our attention to the first great commandment and its implications for the way we speak.

Our words are just as important in our relationship with God as they are in our relationships with one another. One of the ten commandments actually forbids speaking about God in an inappropriate manner: "You shall not take the name of the Lord your God in vain" (Ex 20:7). Just as our words can destroy human relationships, so our words can destroy our relationship with the holy Lord. However, the converse also applies: just as our words can build up and strengthen human relationships, so they can build up and strengthen our relationship with God and others' relationships with God.

Ultimately our tongues have the same purpose as every other part of our life and every portion of our resources: to help us to love, serve, and glorify our Maker and Redeemer. This is the ultimate goal of every faithful Christian's life:

> In him, according to the purpose of him who accomplishes all things according to the counsel of his will, we who first hoped in Christ have been *destined and appointed to live for the praise of his glory.* (Eph 1:11-12)

We succeed in living as a Christian to the extent that we succeed in living fully for the glory of God. There is no higher criterion of action, no loftier purpose or aspiration, no pursuit possessing greater value. Our call to live for the glory of God should shape every aspect of our life—including our speech.

Scripture presents us with many ways in which we can glorify God with our speech. Let us single out five of the most important and examine each of them briefly. Our main sourcebook will be the New Testament and the book of Psalms.

1. Praising God

Praising God is the most direct form of giving him glory. When we offer to God the praise of our lips we are doing more than simply expressing our feelings toward him. In essence, the meaning of our praise is captured best by the very word "offering"; it is an objective gift or sacrifice (in the Old Testament sense), a pleasing aroma before the Lord. Of course, God does not *need* our gift of praise any more than he *needed* the animal sacrifices of the Old Covenant (see Ps 50:10-13). Our praise is not given to inflate his ego or assuage his insecurity. Instead, we offer praise to God because he is infinitely worthy of praise: "Praise is *due* to thee, O God, in Zion" (Ps 65:1a). We owe God the praise of our lips because of the greatness of his wisdom, goodness, and power.

The very fact that we are able to offer a gift to God and have it accepted is his gift to us. He did not have to give us anything, yet he bestowed on us the power of speech. It is only fitting that we use the gift of speech to glorify him. He does not have to receive the gift; like an ancient oriental monarch, he has the right to show his displeasure with us by refusing to accept the offering. Yet God instead chooses to honor our small gifts of praise offered through Jesus Christ, taking pleasure in us as his children and showing us his favor. We read in Psalm 51:15: "O Lord, open thou my lips, and my mouth shall show forth thy praise." Our ability to praise God is thus tied directly to his work in opening our lips. Our ability to offer him a gift of praise is part of his gift to us.

The psalms teach us many things about how we should praise God. According to the psalms, the primary features of our praise should be joy and exuberance:

> Rejoice in the Lord, O you righteous!
>   Praise befits the upright.
> Praise the Lord with the lyre,
>   make melody to him with the harp of ten
>   strings!
> Sing to him a new song,
>   play skilfully on the strings, with loud shouts.
>   (Ps 33:1-3)

> Clap your hand, all peoples!
>   Shout to God with loud songs of joy! . . .
> God has gone up with a shout,
>   the Lord with the sound of a trumpet.
> Sing praises to God, sing praises!
>   Sing praises to our King, sing praises!
>   (Ps 47:1, 5-6)

> Make a joyful noise to God, all the earth;
>   sing the glory of his name;
>   give to him glorious praise! . . .
> All the earth worships thee;

they sing praises to thee,
  sing praises to thy name. (Ps 66:1-2, 4)

O come, let us sing to the Lord;
  let us make a joyful noise to the rock of our
    salvation!
Let us come into his presence with thanks-
    giving;
  let us make a joyful noise to him with songs of
    praise! (Ps 95:1-2)

If we have tasted the goodness of the Lord, then
our lips will not stutter his praises but will instead
flow "like the pen of a ready scribe" (Ps 45:1). The
Lord our God is a great King, and he has lavished
great favors upon us his people; a living personal
knowledge of this truth must lead to some form of
joyful, exuberant praise.

The psalms also show that our praise should not
be sputtering and sporadic, but continual:

I will bless the Lord at all times;
  his praise shall continually be in my mouth.

My soul makes its boast in the Lord;
  let the afflicted hear and be glad.
O magnify the Lord with me,
  and let us exalt his name together! (Ps 34:1-3)

So I will bless thee as long as I live;
  I will lift up my hands and call on thy name.
My soul is feasted as with marrow and fat,
  and my mouth praises thee with joyful lips.
                                        (Ps 63:4-5)

I will extol thee, my God and King,
 and bless thy name for ever and ever.
Every day I will bless thee,
 and praise thy name for ever and ever.
                    (Ps 145:1-2)

As the fire on the altar of the temple and the flame in the lamp were to burn continually, so the praise and worship of the Lord should well up within us continually. And as the priests sacrificed burnt offerings on the altar every morning and every evening as a continual offering before the Lord, so we should take special time each day to do nothing but offer God our sacrifice of praise. It is not enough to praise God on Sunday; he is worthy of praise every day. It is not enough to worship fervently for a few years, and then fade off into a sleepy distraction for a few more. God is worthy of fervent praise every year of our life.

2. Thanking God

Much that was said about praising God also applies to thanking God. Thanksgiving is also an offering, a sacrifice, and scripture teaches that it also is to be offered continually. The difference between the two is subtle, but it is nonetheless important. Praise is offered to God in recognition of the greatness of his attributes—his wisdom, goodness, and power, his righteousness and holiness. Thanksgiving is offered in grateful response to God's merciful concern for our lives. He has created us and redeemed us, he sustains us, and he will glorify us. The only proper response is to honor him with our lips and offer him thanks.

There are several New Testament passages which emphasize the call to regularly offer thanksgiving to God:

And do not get drunk with wine, for that is debauchery; but be filled with the Spirit, addressing one another in psalms and hymns and spiritual songs, singing and making melody to the Lord with all your heart, *always and for everything giving thanks in the name of our Lord Jesus Christ to God the Father*. (Eph 5:18-20)

Let the word of Christ dwell in you richly, teach and admonish one another in all wisdom, and sing psalms and hymns and spiritual songs *with thanksgiving in your hearts to God*. And whatever you do, in word or deed, do everything in the name of the Lord Jesus, *giving thanks to God the Father through him*. (Col 3:16-17)

Rejoice always, pray constantly, *give thanks in all circumstances*; for this is the will of God in Christ Jesus for you. (1 Thes 5:16-18)

The fundamental note of the Christian life is one of thanksgiving. We have been redeemed through the blood of Jesus Christ, we have been filled with the Holy Spirit, we have been adopted into the family of God; we now enjoy full access to the Father through our faith in the Son, and we rejoice in our hope of sharing the glory of God forever. In addition to all of this, we daily experience manifold expressions of his providential care—food, drink, clothing, shelter, family, friends, and even discipline, chastisement, and testing (given for our benefit). Our response to all of this should be to give thanks. We should thank him generally for all the good he has done for us, but we should also thank him specifically for each of the gifts we receive as we receive them. Thus we offer thanks for our food before eating, for our sleep as we go to rest at night, for the coming day as we rise. This is what it means to give thanks "always and for everything" and "in all circumstances."

Many of us fall into the habit of taking our material and spiritual benefits for granted. Our sense of gratitude is dulled by the unspoken conviction that we have rights over the good that has been given us—time, money, job, leisure, abilities, or even our personal relationship with God. When we allow ourselves to fall into such a disposition, we fail to give God the glory he deserves. On the other hand, a grateful heart and a thankful tongue will usually issue in a God-glorifying life.

3. Calling upon the Lord

Another way of giving glory to God with our speech is to call upon his help in times of special need. Calling on the Lord's help glorifies him because it acknowledges him as the beneficent

source of our protection, provision, and susten
ance. We show our confidence in the Lord when
we look to him and call upon his aid.

The psalms are filled with the cries of men who
called out to the Lord:

Hear my cry, O God,
    listen to my prayer;
From the end of the earth I call to thee,
    when my heart is faint.

Lead thou me
    to the rock that is higher than I;
for thou art my refuge,
    a strong tower against the enemy. (Ps 61:1-3)

I love the Lord, because he has heard
    my voice and my supplications.
Because he inclined his ear to me,
    therefore I will call on him as long as I live.
The snares of death encompassed me;
    the pangs of Sheol laid hold of me;
    I suffered distress and anguish.
Then I called on the name of the Lord:
    "O Lord, I beseech thee, save my life!"
                                    (Ps 116:1-4)

I call upon thee, O Lord;
    make haste to me!
    Give ear to my voice, when I call to thee!
Let my prayer be counted as incense before
        thee,
    and the lifting up of my hands as an evening
        sacrifice! (Ps 141:1-2)

When we pray these psalms with sincerity and faith, we confess that our limited human resources are inadequate to meet our needs. We must come to the rock that is higher than we are, the one who is a refuge and a strong tower for his people. In the very act of bringing our petition to the King, we acknowledge him as the true Sovereign whose storehouses overflow with bounty and whose will triumphs over all.

It is possible to call on the Lord in a way that does not glorify him. Sometimes we complain before him like whining children who are totally preoccupied with their own willful desires and are unable to submit to parental discipline. Sometimes we try to manipulate God into backing our own plans. Sometimes we call upon him with anxiety and mistrust, possessing little faith that God hears our prayers as a loving Father eager to provide for his children's needs. Sometimes our relationship with him is dominated by our petitions and leaves little room for praise, worship, thanksgiving, and humble adoration. All such patterns fail to bring glory to God. However, a humble petition offered in faith and confidence comes before him as pleasing incense or an evening sacrifice, and confesses that he is the Sovereign of the universe and the giver of all good gifts.

4. Proclaiming God's Glory to Others

This way of giving glory to God with our speech overlaps with Paul's exhortations to build one another up in love. What better way to build up a brother or sister in Christ than to speak with them directly about the goodness and glory of our King? What better way to love a non-Christian than to speak with him about the One whose salvation extends to all the nations of the earth?

Though speaking of God's glory is upbuilding to others, this is not the only reason for doing it. To speak of God's glory is also an important way of honoring him. As one can honor a human being either by praising him directly or by praising him to a third party, so our speaking to others of God's glory honors him as much as the worship we offer him directly. This is why the psalms summon us to declare God's glory to the nations:

> Sing to the Lord, bless his name;
> tell of his salvation from day to day.
> Declare his glory among the nations,
> his marvelous works among all the peoples!
> (Ps 96:2-3)

> O give thanks to the Lord, call on his name,
> make known his deeds among the peoples!
> Sing to him, sing praises to him,
> tell of all his wonderful works! (Ps 105:1-2)

To speak of God's glory is to give his name the honor it is due. Read Psalm 145, one of the classic passages declaring God's greatness and goodness. No matter how brilliant our eloquence nor how lengthy our treatment, our speech could never hope to exhaust a fraction of his glory or give him the honor that he fully deserves. But we still should do what we are able to do, though our praises be incommensurate to the worth of their object.

The scripture especially urges us to proclaim God's salvation, the acts of deliverance he has accomplished on our behalf. Psalm 71:15 tells us that we should declare the Lord's salvation all the day:

> My mouth will tell of thy righteous acts,
>   of thy deeds of salvation all the day,
>   for their number is past my knowledge.

In the New Testament, 1 Peter 2:9 shows us that such a declaration is integral to our mission as the people of God:

> But you are a chosen race, a royal priesthood, a holy nation, God's own people, that you may declare the wonderful deeds of him who called you out of darkness into his marvelous light.

This is true in a general sense; we should speak to one another about the awesome grace of God revealed in the incarnation of Jesus Christ and his self-offering upon the cross, and about all the boundless favors of God manifested to us in the scripture. However, it is also true in a more particular sense; we should speak to one another of the specific ways that God has acted in our lives to deliver us from bondage and lead us into his kingdom. Such specific testimonies to God's salvation are found in several places in the psalms:

> I will tell of thy name to my brethren;
>> in the midst of the congregation I will praise thee:
>
> You who fear the Lord, praise him!
>> all you sons of Jacob, glorify him,
>> and stand in awe of him, all you sons of Israel!
>
> For he has not despised or abhorred
>> the affliction of the afflicted;
>
> and he has not hid his face from him,
>> but has heard, when he cried to him.
>
> (Ps 22:22-24)

> I have told the glad news of deliverance
>> in the great congregation;
>
> lo, I have not restrained my lips,
>> as thou knowest, O Lord.
>
> I have not hid thy saving help within my heart.
>> I have spoken of thy faithfulness and thy salvation;
>
> I have not concealed thy steadfast love and thy faithfulness
>> from the great congregation. (Ps 40:9-10)

After healing a demoniac, Jesus commissioned him to go home and glorify God by telling how he was healed. Jesus called him to follow the model established in Psalms 22 and 40:

> The man from whom the demons had gone
> begged that he might be with him; but he sent
> him away, saying, "Return to your home, and
> declare how much God has done for you." And
> he went away, proclaiming throughout the
> whole city how much Jesus had done for him.
> (Lk 8:38-39)

These words of Jesus also apply to us. He has
healed us by his power and delivered us from
demonic oppression. It is therefore only fitting
that we share with others the good news of what
God has done in our lives.

It is possible to speak to others about the glory
of God and fail in the attempt. Sometimes we
merely repeat vague, hackneyed, pious cliches that
fail to express what we have actually experienced.
Sometimes we speak in a way that draws attention
to ourselves rather than to the Lord. Sometimes
we talk to non-Christians about the Lord in such
thick religious jargon that they cannot understand
what we are saying and have no desire to find out.
These pitfalls should not intimidate and discourage us, but should instead make us eager to
couple wisdom with zeal in our efforts to proclaim
the glory of God.

5. Confessing Jesus

A final important way to glorify God with our
speech is urged upon us by the New Testament
with special solemnity—the confession of faith in

Jesus Christ in the face of opposition and testing.
The ultimate confession is martyrdom, which in
Greek simply means testimony or witness. In the
early church, those who suffered for their faithful
testimony but were not killed were called "con-
fessors" and given special honor. This type of
speech—unlike those previously mentioned—is
not a daily occurrence. Nonetheless, the way we
handle ourselves daily determines whether we
pass the test on the day it comes.

In the middle of his teaching on discipleship
and persecution in the tenth chapter of Matthew,
Jesus speaks these sobering words about con-
fessing him in the face of opposition:

> So every one who acknowledges me before men,
> I also will acknowledge before my Father who is
> in heaven; but whoever denies me before men, I
> also will deny before my Father who is in
> heaven. (Mt 10:32-33)

If we acknowledge loyally before men that Jesus is
our Master and Lord, heedless of the consequences, undaunted by the cost, then Jesus will
acknowledge before all the company of heaven
that we are his faithful disciples and servants. This
passage is often used to emphasize the importance
of evangelism, but that is not its primary purpose.
Its primary purpose is to deal with the pressure on
the disciple to deny—overtly or covertly—his
relationship with his Master. The question raised
here is one of loyalty: "Will you faithfully and

loyally confess your relationship with me, even when the consequences are likely to be painful?" Peter found himself in such a situation on the eve of the crucifixion, and he failed the test. Jesus gave him many other opportunities later on to take the test again, and Peter passed with flying colors, as recorded in the book of Acts.

Another example of a man who passed the test with flying colors is Polycarp, a second-century bishop from the city of Smyrna in Asia Minor. An old man, Polycarp was hustled before the proconsul in the arena and pressed to deny the Lord Jesus:

> The Governor, however, still went on pressing him. "Take the oath, and I will let you go," he told him. "Revile your Christ." Polycarp's reply was, "Eighty and six years have I served Him, and He has done me no wrong. How then can I blaspheme my King and my Saviour?"

Polycarp gives us a sterling model of a man whose loyalty to Jesus is expressed by the words he speaks in the time of testing. He died as he had lived—in fidelity to the one who had first died for him.

Few of us will probably ever face such a dramatic test. However, we all have smaller tests—situations in which our acknowledging Jesus costs us something in loss of acceptance, respect, or position. These become our "arenas," our opportunities to show our colors. If we are living fully for the glory of God, our lips will confess Jesus in that day, heedless of the cost, glorifying God with bridled tongues consecrated to the worship and service of his name.

The Glorious Tongue

Scripture calls us to love the Lord our God with our whole heart, mind, and soul. We also need to love the Lord with our tongue. The tongue is not just a mischievous nuisance that always gets us into trouble; it is a gift from God of tremendous power and nobility, able to speak words of salvation and build up the people of God in love, able to sing with the angels of the glory and goodness of the heavenly King. Let us all treat this gift with the respect it deserves, and devote it fully to the service of its merciful Giver.

The books in the Living as a Christian series can be used effectively in groups. A *Study Guide* for using all of the Living as a Christian books in groups is available from Servant. To order, send $3.00 plus $.75 for postage to Servant Book Express, Box 8617, Ann Arbor, Michigan 48107.